RISING
Above

THE LORENZO WASHINGTON STORY

Lorenzo Washington

PUBLISHING, LLC

Best · 2. Washington

Lorenzo Washington

JSSM Publishing, LLC
Madison, TN 37115

Publisher: JSSM Publishing, LLC
Project Manager: Sedrik Newbern, Newbern Consulting, LLC
Editor: Linda Wolf, Network Publishing Partners, Inc.
Cover Designer: M Hurley, Teknigram Graphics, Inc.

Printed in the United States of America
First Edition: June 2021

ISBN Paperback: 978-1-7359746-0-6

Library of Congress Control Number: 2021907466

Dedication

This is dedicated to my children.

You are my rock.

Table of Contents

Chapter 1
Wichita Street

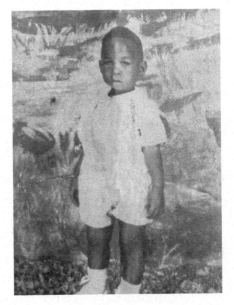

My baby picture

When I came into the world on January 31, 1943, my family lived in a small, 4-room house in East Nashville, Tennessee. I was raised up in that house until I was 14 years old.

I don't remember my dad being around much while I was growing up. All I really knew of him was his name, Thomas Washington, and his nickname, Nug. But I had plenty of family to love in that little old red house on Wichita Street. Under the tin roof lived my mother, Julia Washington, my grandmother Nellie Davis, my grandfather Gerley Davis, and my uncle Fred Litton, for starters. I was the firstborn of four brothers, and I remember the whole family – my mother's sisters and brothers, everybody – congregated there, because it was my grandmother's house.

The house had two fireplaces in its four rooms, along with a coal heater and a cooking stove in the kitchen. My mother had one of the rooms with her four boys. She slept in one bed with my little baby brother, and the other three of us slept in the bed next to them. A coal fireplace heated that room. My grandmother slept in the front room on the other side of our room. Granddaddy slept in the back room, and my uncle slept in the kitchen on a little cot that he would pull out at night.

The houses in our neighborhood were not close together but were small wood-framed houses with linoleum floors and no running water. So, there were no kitchen sinks – instead we had dishpans we used for washing dishes from water we carried in. Kerosene lamps were used for light. Our walls were covered with floral wallpaper that we replaced with new wallpaper every Christmas. The houses had front porches that stretched the full width of the front of the house, and there was enough land between each house for the kids to freely play. The neighborhood took up about 10 blocks including 5 streets: Wichita, Cowan, Berry, Turner, and Cowan Street Alley. Some of these streets no longer exist due to the expansion of the interstate.

One strong memory from those early years was when the backwater would come up and invade the whole neighborhood. This happened about every two or three years.

"Fats! We've got to clear out. The water's coming again!" my mother would shout. They called me Fats because I was a huge 12-pound baby at birth and spent some time as the little fat boy in the family until I got taller. When that water was coming, we wouldn't have much warning, and the entire neighborhood would mobilize in a hurry. The water would eventually rise all the way up to waist-high on an adult, and we would have to clear everything out of the house.

Once the backwater went back down, we had to go in and scrub the walls down, get the mud out, and clean it up. Then we'd move right back in. The city had a special truck they would send in during those times that we used to call a boat. It was an amphibious truck that would go in the water and also on land. We kids used to get pretty excited about that "boat."

Since we had no running water inside the house, we had to carry it from the hydrant that was about 10 feet from the back door. We had an outhouse that was probably 60 feet from the house. The world was at war when I was born, but by the time I was school-aged, the post-war boom was in full swing, and many neighborhoods in Nashville were upgrading. New houses with all the latest conveniences seemed to spring up overnight, but our neighborhood on Wichita Street went on unchanged, without running water, protection from flooding, or any assistance from the City of Nashville to improve the quality of life. We didn't get electricity until I was about 12.

My paternal grandmother Isabelle "Big Mama" Washington had running water, though. My brothers and I would spend some weekends at her house. She lived with my grandfather, Thomas Washington, and our Aunt Ernestine in a small house on Mark Street. Big Mama would cook breakfast for the family, and we would take nice warm baths in her bathtub. In our own house on Wichita, we had to take baths in an old metal tub, so of course we wanted to take baths at Big Mama's house. Plus, it was a nice place to be on the weekends – Mark Street was a community with other kids who enjoyed riding bikes, skating, and shooting marbles.

My mother was one of the mothers of the neighborhood. Everybody knew her and called her "Aunt Julia." I also called her Julia, never "Mother" or "Mama," though I don't know how I got to calling her by her first name. It was always just Julia. She was a very sweet lady – in fact I look more like my mother than any of the other boys do. My personality and disposition were closest to hers, too. Being the oldest of her sons, I was the one she would call on to help the neighbors.

"Look out for the older folk in the neighborhood," she would say. "Go to the store for the little ladies down the street." If one of the older ladies needed her grass cut, my mother would send me. She elected me to do those things because that's the kind of person she was, and she knew she could get that out of me, too, to learn to do for others.

My grandfather, Gerley Davis, was a hardworking man. He would leave for work at 4 or 5 in the morning and get off at 4 or 5 in the evening. He worked for a company that sold wallboards, cement, sand, and other heavy construction products. He was the warehouse attendant, so he was the one unloading the boxcars when they brought supplies in. We used to go down as kids and help him unload the boxcars. I remember him going down to the warehouse at night, and we would go in there with him to pull the trash, but he would never turn the lights on. I still remember that. I don't know why he wouldn't turn those lights on. So, we would pull the trash with him and clean the bathrooms in the dark.

But that was my grandfather – he was a good old man. He was from up around the Springfield area. His granddad was a slave. I remember my mother getting some funds from the sale of some land that my granddaddy owned along with his cousins and brothers and all. That land was given to his own granddaddy right after slavery. We've all heard about "40 acres and a mule" – well, his family actually got 40 acres and a mule! Granddaddy sold off some of the land, so the family got together and sold 25 acres. My mother got $4,000 from that sale.

There were cousins and aunts and uncles scattered around Michigan and up around Detroit, because they all migrated to the north right after slavery. That's where most of them were. But my granddad stayed put in Tennessee and was a humble old man. He worked such long hours that we didn't actually see him a lot outside of the house. He would come home and wash up in a little wash pan, since we didn't have running water in the house.

Granddad always took good care of his family. He provided for our mother and her four sons, my grandmother, and my mother's three sisters. Whenever one of the sisters had problems with their boyfriends or husbands, they would all come to the house. Sometimes in that little 4-room house, there were as many as 10 or 12 people making pallets to sleep.

Since I was the oldest in my family, it became my role to be one of the most responsible kids helping the grownups. One of my aunts had a mental disability, and my mother needed to step in at times and help with her five kids. I was always the one going with my mother to take my aunt to the hospital or help look after the kids when she stayed in the hospital.

There were times when we needed to take my aunt to the mental hospital, and the police would have to come for her when my mother couldn't handle her. It was upsetting to the family to see the police restrain my aunt to take her to the hospital. We went through a lot of things with our family, but we were very close. My brothers and I still, to this day, do things for each other and see each other often.

We had an uncle living in our house who was an alcoholic, but he wasn't a bad person at all. He would run and play with the kids when we teased and kidded with him. We would antagonize him at times, calling him funny names and running from him just so he would chase after us.

Every weekend, Granddad would get dressed up sharp. My grandmother would iron one of his best shirts until it looked like it came out of a professional laundry. He would put on elegant striped pants with suspenders and a fancy Stetson hat, tilting it carefully to just the right angle as he stood before the mirror in Grandma's room. We kids would watch these preparations in fascination.

He put on this outfit every Saturday and went to the beer joint, and some weekends he would get drunk. Then my mother and I would have to go down in the alley to get him, literally pick him up and carry him from the beer joint to home. He was a big, strong man, and we would have to set him down four or five times before we got home.

Everybody knew everybody's business in the neighborhood, so whenever we needed help, the neighbors would pitch in to get Granddad safely home. This beer joint was down in Cowan Street alley, and we had to get him all the way from there back to Wichita Street.

My grandmother, Nellie Davis, can trace her lineage back to her great grandfather, Richard Love. Richard Love had five children and one was my great grandmother, Mattie White Jones. Mattie only birthed one child, Nellie. Nellie had four daughters: Rosetta Smith, Julia Washington(my mother), Dorothy Allison, and Mamie Horton. Aunt Rosetta was called Roselle, and she was the artist in the family. She sang at church functions, so all the community knew her. She called me her favorite nephew. Aunt Mamie was a real entrepreneur and she had a T-model Ford called Aunt Molly. Her oldest son Clifford and I learned how to drive in that car up and down the alley, stealing it away while Aunt Mamie was busy visiting at our house.

Grandma slept in the front room with my cousin Bobby. My grandmother pretty much raised him because her youngest daughter, my Aunt Dorothy, was having so many problems with her husband. Bobby was one day older than me – my mother and his mother were two sisters in the same hospital room at one point, to give birth and bring us into the world.

We were all kind of jealous of Bobby because Grandma would buy him new bicycles, skates, and clothes. But our mother had to get us stuff from the Salvation Army. If we got a bicycle, skates, clothes, or toys, they were all used. My mother could always put something under the tree for us, but we remembered Bobby getting a brand-new bicycle under the tree in my grandmother's room.

My grandmother was a great cook, and she would do any-thing she could for any of us kids. On that old coal stove in the kitchen, my grandmother used to cook these biscuits. She could make some of the best biscuits on that coal stove that you'd ever taste. And cakes! She was just a magician in the kitchen.

I always wanted to help the grownups in our family. For Christmas when I was a little kid, 7 or 8 years old, I would haul coal and wood for some of the neighbors so that I could get enough money to buy presents for my mother and my grandmother. My mother smoked cigarettes. I knew it would make her happy to receive a pack of cigarettes. So, I would hustle enough money to get her a pack of cigarettes for Christmas. My grandmother liked snuff. So, I would get her a box of Garrett's snuff.

I had been going to the neighborhood store since I was 5 years old with a little note to pick up whatever my mother or my grandmother wanted from the store. The storeowner knew me well and would sell cigarettes and snuff to me for them. Every so often, my mother drank RC Cola and I would go get her an RC. It made me feel so proud to be able to get them those Christmas presents every year.

That little store was two doors down from us and across the street on Wichita. I went to that store to pick up things for my family starting in 1948 all the way up until we moved out when I was 14, in 1957. You would always see people from the neighborhood in there. It was just a tiny store carrying little essentials like cold drinks, potato chips, and milk. I can still remember the little bundles of kindling to start fires with; they were set up at the side of the door when you first walked in. Just about everybody had a coal stove or a wood fireplace back then.

Mr. Whittaker, the gentleman running the store, knew just about every kid in the neighborhood by name. I'm sure he had been there since I was born, and probably way before. But he knew all of the kids. Once in a while, we would go in there and not have enough money to get everything we were sent to get. He would give us what we came to get and write a little note to take back to our parents so they would know we were a dime short or fifteen cents short. When we did get the money, my family would send me back with that dime or fifteen cents, and our credit was good.

Every so often, Mr. Whittaker would have us sweep up around out in front of the store. I remember sweeping up and getting a piece of candy or a sack of potato chips or something. We hardly ever got any money for doing chores around the store, but we'd always get something. And that would be satisfying to a kid, to get candy or chips or a cookie or a peppermint. That was an experience doing that.

Our house was a popular place for the neighborhood kids. There was an empty field next door to our house where we built a basketball court of sorts. We made the rim from a fruit basket that was used for apples. We nailed that fruit basket to the backboard of the goal we put up in the field. All of the kids congregated in this field. Every evening, that was the place to go. We didn't have community centers and that kind of thing back then, but we did have that field next door. We would play basketball until you couldn't see the ball anymore.

It was a lot of fun for all the kids in the neighborhood. Just about every house had at least 3, 4, or 5 kids. There were a couple of houses with 12 or 14 kids. There were a lot of kids in the community, especially by the time I was 10 years old and up.

Some of the outstanding perks I got out of life involved being able to help the women in our community. It was mostly mothers and grandmothers, and very few fathers, in the neighborhood. There was one father, Mr. Owen Hunter, who had something like 14 kids. My best friend, Herbert Hunter, was one of his sons. Mr. Hunter was a minister, but he was also like a father to the neighborhood. He was a short guy, but he had plenty of respect from all of the kids.

We had a very loving life growing up, but we didn't have a lot of material things, and we didn't have very much money at all. Despite the lack of money and some hard times, those childhood years were full of laughter and fun in our extended family and our community.

Chapter 2
Making My Way

With my brothers James "Peewee" Washington
(left) and Ernest "Seemore" Washington (right):
Still best friends after all these years

When I was 14 years old, we moved to a housing project in
the Sam Levy Homes projects. We all called it Settle Court
because that was the name of our street. There were 300-
400 apartment units. This was off Lischey Avenue, walking
distance from our old house. Moving into that three-
bedroom housing project apartment felt like moving into a
mansion because we had running water, hot water, and
electric lights. We didn't have to clean the lampshades and
fill the lamps up with kerosene in order to have light at
night. What a difference to just hit a switch and have lights!

That was a transitional time for me and my brothers, being able to live a better life with my grandparents and my mother. The Salvation Army was still where my mother used to buy just about all of our clothes and shoes. I remember I could never get a pair of shoes that actually fit me. I usually had to get shoes that were a little too tight because I had big feet back then (and still do). The best-looking shoes we could find at the Salvation Army were donated by men with little feet, apparently. To this day, I still have problems with corns on both feet because of wearing shoes that were too small when I was growing up.

In my teen years, I started working every chance I got. When I made enough money to actually buy new shoes, they came from Boyd's Shoe Store downtown. I was always a shoe person and I still am. My mother was the same way; she was a person who loved shoes. Once I started working more hours at my various jobs, I loved being able to buy my own shoes and clothes. I've always hustled for myself and my family. In order to work enough hours, I didn't go to school for 30 or 40 days out of a school year. I would play hooky and go to work.

My brothers weren't as active about trying to get ahead as I was. My next brother in age, who is no longer living, was Thomas Washington, nicknamed Tink. We all had nicknames. The brother after him is Ernest Washington – we call him Seemore. Our youngest brother is James

Washington, called Peewee. We were all about two years apart from each other.

Tink was a lady's man – good-looking, standing at 6'2, charming, and reliable – all the characteristics that the women loved. We miss him to this day. He died around age 25 in a tragic accident while driving a truck on his job.

Seemore was a kind little boy and always helpful to everybody in the neighborhood. Like me, he was busy cutting grass, bringing in coal, and getting groceries for people at an early age. He was an excellent cook and loved cooking for the entire family. This talent of his has followed him all through life. When I had a barbecue business later on, he was one of the cooks.

Peewee was a momma's boy and hung around our mother a lot. She did not want him getting in trouble with the bad kids in the neighborhood and was very protective of her youngest boy. He loved to dance and was the best dancer in the family.

With no father around to help out, I felt responsible for helping my mother make ends meet and provide for all five of us. I would take a job doing all kinds of things. I worked with the market men or on the "banana truck" that delivered fruits and vegetables to the residents of East Nashville. I also worked with the men driving around the coal and ice wagon. They would deliver coal and ice to houses in the community and I would be up on the back of one of those horse-drawn wagons instead of in school.

I never was into learning. It seemed like that never was my interest – looking for a way to make money was my primary interest. So, I did it pretty well, considering where I came from.

I got a job at Lonnie Young's Shoe Repair downtown on Third Avenue in 1955 when I was 12 years old. The boss thought that instead of just shining shoes, I could deliver shoes once they were repaired. Lonnie Young's hired me to deliver shoes to department stores like Cain-Sloan, Castner Knott, Grace's Shoes, and Harvey's.

I've never been able to read very well at all, and I couldn't read the names on all of those stores. So, I developed a little number system for each store, and I used that to figure out where I was supposed to take each pair of shoes. I would never tell my bosses that I couldn't read. Lonnie Young's taught me more than just delivering. I was so ambitious that they taught me how to turn a finishing machine on and finish the heels and soles on the shoes. At 12 years old, there I was standing over a machine with my little apron on finishing the shoes and getting ready to put the dye on the soles. That was a big deal for me – rather than just shining shoes or delivering shoes, I learned how to finish shoes.

It was an eye-opening experience working downtown and being able to see all the busy folk rushing around. I would go past the real shoeshine parlors downtown on 4th Avenue, Nickerson's and others, where the older guys stood out in front and hustled customers inside to get their shoes shined. I would go up to 4th Avenue to watch how they worked the crowds, bringing in customers for a shoeshine. That's where I learned a lot about how to attract customers in off the street. Even at 12, I was already trying to take things to the next level. People noticed that I was that kind of guy.

I worked at Lonnie Young's for about a year, and then I landed my first long-term regular job at Hoover's Amoco Gas Station. I started out at age 13 washing cars there at the service station. My best friend from childhood, Herbert Hunter, was working there and helped me land the job. Mr. Hoover, the old gentleman who owned the gas station, used to call me "George" because of my last name, Washington, and often said that I would never tell a lie (like George Washington). He was fond of me. They called me his pet. He always had me over at his house doing things while the rest of the guys were out there washing cars and fixing flat tires.

As I got older, I worked in the evenings with the owner's son, Billy. Unlike his father, Billy Hoover was a very negative, aggressive guy. We all called him a redneck behind his back. He was different from most of the other white people we knew, especially the ones from around the neighborhood. They didn't treat us the way he did.

Billy Hoover had been in the army, and when he got back home, I was around 14 years old and well established as a trusted employee of his father. Right away, Billy swaggered around acting like the king of the neighborhood because he had learned a few things about combat and fighting in the service. He thought he was a real tough guy, wearing his shirt collar high up on his neck like he was bad stuff. He acted like he could come into the station and whoop any of his father's Black employees that he felt like whooping. He called us a lot of ugly, ugly names and used the N word a lot, always cussing at us.

At night, he would have us cleaning the shelves, wiping off the oil cans, and straightening up inside. He would go into the bathroom to make sure the mirrors were clean and the walls and fixtures spotless, and if they weren't, there would be hell to pay. Sometimes a cop on duty would pull up to the pump and we wouldn't immediately see that car because he had us so busy cleaning inside. If there was any kind of delay for us in getting out there to pump gas for the cop, Billy would come up banging on the side door, calling us the N word, "you Black this, you Black that," and carrying on so he could show off what a powerful man he was to the police.

At the time, I needed the money so badly that I would accept whatever he said. He could talk however he liked to me as long as I could walk out of there at night with my 50 cents. That 50 cents had to serve as lunch money for me and my three brothers, so I needed it.

The same year that Billy got back from the army, Mr. Hoover got cancer and became very sick. That's when old Mr. Hoover had me come over more and more often to do things around the house for him and his wife. As he got weaker from the cancer, it got to the point where he would need me to carry him to the bathroom or be moved around in the house, and I would pick him up and set him on a chair or in the bathroom. I would carry him from the bedroom to the kitchen and sit him down at the table so his wife could feed him. He got down to weighing 60 or 70 pounds.

I became a caretaker to Mr. Hoover, and he was grateful to me. He treated me with kindness and respect. He nailed a little cigar box to a top shelf in his house so that it wouldn't fall off, and where it was high enough that I could barely reach it. That was how he taught me to save money. I would reach up and put part of the money I made every night into this cigar box. When I was making 50 cents a night, I would put a dime or 15 cents in his cigar box some nights when I had gotten a tip.

I eventually got up to 50 cents an hour instead of 50 cents a night. A lot of nights I would get at least a dime or a 15-cent tip at the end of the night. I was pretty good at getting the tips back then at the station, because if you were courteous and kind and helpful to folks, they would be helpful back to you.

I ended up doing just about everything for old man Hoover once he became unable to walk at all. Billy never appreciated the things I did for the old man, but the old man appreciated me. Once his father was unable to come into the store anymore, then Billy was totally in charge. There was no one to stop him now, and he really got down hard on us after that.

The day finally came when I turned 16 and he walked up to look me in the eye as usual, calling me those ugly names. Up to that day, I would just turn and walk away from him to avoid a confrontation. But now I was 16 years old, and I had had enough. When he walked up, looked down at me, and started cussing, I just stood there. I didn't say a word, but I didn't walk away or look away – just stared right back at him, eye to eye. I was ready to tackle him that day because I had reached my limit.

Something changed in his face in that moment, and from then on, he stopped confronting me and calling me names. Eventually, I moved on to bigger things and left that job when I was 18 and old Mr. Hoover passed away. But Billy Hoover stayed on at that gas station, year after year, treating the other young Black kids the same way he had treated me.

Years later, about the time I was 44 years old, he was 55 or 60. I decided it was time to pay the old station a visit. There was Billy Hoover working at the station that day, and I pulled up in a brand-new Saab 9000 Turbo, a beautiful car. I threw the car door open with the music playing. When I got out of the car, he didn't know who I was at first. He said, "Can I help you?"

"Yes," I said, with a little smile to myself. "Fill it up."

He stared at me. "Fats?!"

"Yeah," I answered and leaned against the car to watch him fill it up. That was a good day.

While Billy filled the car up with gas, I enjoyed watching him admire the Saab. It was white with a light gray interior, and a very expensive car at that time. I owned a cleaning company by then, and Thoroughbred Motors was one of my big clients, so they worked a deal for me to get that car.

A few years after that, I heard that Billy Hoover ended up hanging himself in the same bathroom that I used to clean all the time while he cussed us out about every little speck of dirt. It was reported that he had about $300,000 in cash in that bathroom when he hung himself. At the end, he must have been as miserable inside as he acted on the outside.

Of all the things, good and bad, that happened to me in my young life, there was one situation with my father that had more emotional impact on me than anything else I can remember from those younger days. My father worked at the Nashville Bridge Company near the Cumberland River. He was supposed to give my mother $15 a week for these four boys that he had. When I was 12, the principal would let me out of school 15 minutes early every Friday so I would have enough time to walk to my father's work before they closed at 3:00.

Once I arrived at the Nashville Bridge Company office, I would sit down in the little lobby on a bench. I remember that bench so well. I would wait there until he got off his shift, went into the locker area, took his shower, and came out. At least 3 weeks out of each month, though, he would go out the back door and leave me sitting on that bench, waiting, until 4 or 4:30 in the evening. I would be sitting there waiting for him to give us that $15, which we desperately needed. One of the janitors would show up finally in the hallway and look at me.

"Boy, are you waiting for your daddy?" he would ask.

"Yes, sir," I said.

"There's nobody left in the building now, son. They're all gone."

And that would just break my heart. To this day, that is one of the saddest memories I carry with me.

Chapter 3
The Challenge of "Making It"

All the kids in my neighborhood went to the same school, Meigs School, from elementary through high school at that time. Getting through school was a lot easier back in those days than it is now. I genuinely liked and respected my teachers, and they liked me so much that they would just pass me on to the next grade. It wasn't because I made good grades – I never turned in papers of any kind or studied for any exams. That's how loose the educational system was at my school.

My teachers liked me because I was such a courteous person. I was obedient and respectful, saying, "Yes, ma'am" and "Yes, sir." We were taught to be that way at home, and I brought that to school. It helped me to get through those years.

There were a few teachers I really liked. One was Mrs. Jordan, my 2nd grade teacher. She was tall and very pretty, and she was truly nice to the students. She was far and away one of the prettiest teachers in the school. Mr. Walker was my homeroom teacher in 7th grade. He and Mr. Gray were the industrial arts teachers. Mr. Gray was the coach for basketball and football. We didn't have a lot of coaches, so usually one or two coaches coached everything back then.

I enjoyed my time with these teachers because I felt I was learning something from them that was going to help me later on in life. I made a table in Mr. Gray's industrial arts class, and he gave me so much praise. He went out of his way to encourage me to come to school more often. Since he was the basketball coach, he brought me on the team. I was one of the first five on the basketball team, and that was exciting. That was in the 10th or 11th grade.

In our school culture, I was looked upon as a guy with a great personality. I was not only respectful to the teachers, but to the young ladies I went to school with. Those young ladies liked me because I was an achiever. I worked hard and bought my first car at 15 years old. There weren't more than one or two other kids driving a car to school back then, so that made me pretty popular. Also, I always dressed nice because I had pride in how I looked. That brought me some notoriety with the other students. I would give 15 or 20 cents to some of the kids to buy lunch if they didn't have lunch money. Little things like that triggered people to say things like, "That's a pretty nice guy there."

I went to school for a number of years thinking that I would be somebody important. But I knew that it would be hard for me to be a class president since I wasn't academically inclined and didn't have the best attendance record, to say the least. I've always been ambitious, reaching for higher, bigger, and better things. So, there I was, a guy who couldn't read or write well, even though I had beautiful handwriting. But I had friends in high places, you might say. One of those friends was the class president, so I took her to the prom. She ended up getting PhD's and all of that later on.

I've always been attracted to people who are smarter than I am. That has been a central factor behind a lot of the things I've done, because I am drawn to the smartest, the brightest, the movers and shakers. I was an achiever, but not in the classroom. The smarter students wanted to be around me and be a part of what I was producing. I was always working on some idea, some project – I'm still that way to this day.

Back then, we weren't into worldly things so much – it was all about the community. It was all about what was happening right around us. To go to a McDonald's (but back then it was Krystal's) was something big, just to get out. I started setting my sights on getting out of the small world of my neighborhood, striving for something bigger and better. In my 11th grade year, I stopped showing up at school. I was working full-time by then fixing tires and washing cars, so it was a trade-off, a necessary trade-off.

Even though I started out at pretty menial jobs, I always found a way to grow to the next level by bringing other folks in with me on my ideas. My passion for teamwork really started later on when I started going into business for myself, but it all got its start back then in high school. I was never accomplished at managing paperwork, but I was a planner. I could bring things together and make things happen, and I knew how to get the right people on board and dedicated to my ideas and plans. In my own way, I was just as smart as those who did well in school, and I was always one of the leaders on the team as I moved into different ventures and situations.

My aim was set high on being a millionaire. I knew I was going to need smart guys, guys who thought being a millionaire was just another expected move in life, so I had to team up with those kinds of people, and I did. I've always been that way. Being Black did not offer up many entrepreneurial opportunities, so I was on the lookout for anything that looked promising and profitable.

Things in my personal life were getting complicated at that point. I was pretty mischievous and confident at 15, hanging out with all these older guys, and I had a very short relationship with a girl who was two or three years older than I was. After this one relationship, a daughter was born. When the baby was born, I didn't think it was my kid at all, but it turned out that the little girl was mine. The child's mother had a boyfriend who became her husband, and he took total responsibility for the baby. I wasn't ready to be a father during those years, so I never had the chance to develop a relationship with that little girl.

Even though I bought my first car when I was 15, I couldn't drive it until I was 16 because I didn't have a driver's license yet. So, I'd get some of the older guys to drive my car, and wherever they went, I went. They would go to the taverns and the clubs, and I would go with them late at night (late at night was 10:00 to 11:00 back then for us). I got a chance to see the excitement of Jefferson Street before I turned 16, just by running with the older guys who had driver's licenses. You didn't see a lot of Black folk in cars around the city at that time, so we felt pretty special.

Jefferson Street was such an exciting place to visit. Since we lived in East Nashville, it was almost like going out of town for us when we were young, coming over to North Nashville to Jefferson Street. It was eye-opening, a real education in city life, to me. We would ride up and down Jefferson Street and hear all the sounds of the live music, people talking and laughing, with everyone dressed in bright colors and moving quickly on the street. Guys and girls would call down to their friends from the balconies and windows of the lounges and the restaurants up and down Jefferson Street.

We saw kids walking to the ice cream parlors, people going to the bakeries, older women going in and out of the churches, and people milling around all the stores on Jefferson Street. Going to Jefferson Street was like going to Broadway in downtown New York City, coming from Wichita Street in Nashville, Tennessee.

The whole area was almost completely Black-owned. A few of the bigger grocery stores were white-owned, and some of the clothing stores had Jewish owners. But the vast majority of all the businesses on Jefferson Street were Black-owned. That's why Jefferson Street at that time was called self-contained. We had all of our own investments over here on Jefferson Street. We invested in the land, we invested in the stores, and we invested in the schools. Jefferson Street was a major investment for the Black community.

I worked a number of jobs during those years. One of the first was at The Krystal on Charlotte Pike. It was a lot like the White Castles we have now. I was the first Black employee to flip hamburgers at The Krystal. That was a big thing for me. I also worked at Channel 8 TV, cleaning their premises. I worked those two jobs at the same time.

At Channel 8 on Saturdays, they aired wrestling matches. One Saturday, Joe Louis, the famous boxer came in. He was just making a hustle as we used to call it. He was over there after Uncle Sam had gotten him for back taxes and he was broke. He was just trying to make some money, so he was over there at the TV station wrestling.

I would go to the back room and he and his opponent would be there practicing how they were going to flip each other and throw each other. It actually broke my heart to see our world champion Joe Louis back there being thrown on a mat wrestling. He was the heavyweight champion of the world in his prime! That was an experience that I couldn't get my head around because Joe Louis was a hero. He was one of our greatest heroes, as far as our community was concerned.

It was degrading to see him in the ring wrestling. Everybody knew wrestling was a fake sport, as we called it. We used to have wrestling in our neighborhood. Seeing Joe Louis in the ring like that was devastating to me.

Then I worked at Cutter's Exchange. I was a shipping and receiving clerk, which was really something unbelievable, because I couldn't read. I could recall words and I could make out certain words enough to get by. I've always been good enough with people that I could help them, and then they would help me to get my work done correctly. I had another shipping and receiving clerk job at Spartans Department Store. I had 26 departments to accept goods in and ship goods out for. How I did it, I couldn't tell you, but I did it for two years.

After that, I worked for the State of Tennessee as an air conditioning and heating operator. Despite all the demanding jobs I held, I never worked at just one job. I always had plans brewing with someone to make more money and kept some kind of side job going to keep lots of irons in the fire.

Chapter 4
Cruisin' Jefferson Street

I was going regularly to Jefferson Street with my friend Herbert Hunter. We grew up together in the old neighborhood, and he was a singer. Through him, I was able to be a part of the music scene on Jefferson Street at the age of 17. During that period, 1959–1960, the sit-ins, marches, and riots for civil rights really started to heat up. I was from East Nashville and I was a local, so I wasn't involved. Usually the only ones involved in the marches and sit-ins were college students.

The civil rights movement had a deep effect on me. I got a chance to see all those people marching and working together for change, and I always wanted to be a part of what these smart college kids were a part of. I felt like I was being left out of a lot because I wasn't as educated. I stood outside the whites-only lunch counter at Woolworth's downtown and watched the white customers push and be ugly to the Black students who sat on the stools. I told my friends that I was going to eventually go inside, sit down, and order some food.

It took a long time for me to get my nerve up to go down and mix and mingle with college kids who were protesting, but I did eventually go down and sit on that forbidden stool.

By that time, the protests were not a new disturbance, and it seemed like the white world was beginning to expect them, if not accept them. I got pushed on the shoulders a few times that day at Woolworth's, but nothing really violent happened. It meant a lot to me to be a part of what the students were going through.

At the same time, I was becoming more and more familiar with the musicians and the people at all of the clubs up and down Jefferson Street. My best friend, Herbert, put out a record with Ted Jarrett that was a bit of a hit. If your music was being played on the radio, you were somebody in this town. When he started singing at different events and different clubs, I was there with him.

Around that time, my son Dwayne was born. I dated Dwayne's mother, Emma Westmoreland, for about 2 or 3 years. She was a very attractive young lady, and we ended up having a son. Until Dwayne was about 3 or 4 years old, I would keep him on the weekends and took care of him financially. By the time Dwayne was 4, I was spending more and more time out there working jobs and making things happen to make money. I didn't have time for a girlfriend anymore. Dwayne was with my mother a lot after that. If Emma had something she needed to do during the week, she would bring Dwayne over to stay with my mother while I was working.

That's when Emma and I drifted apart, when Dwayne was 4 or 5 years old. Emma became involved with Tommy, who went to Pearl High School with her. When Dwayne was 5, Tommy decided that he wanted to raise Dwayne, and he didn't want me to be a part of that. I never wanted to be a threat to Tommy. All I wanted was to be a part of my son's life, but Tommy could offer him what I couldn't at that time – family life. I turned my attention to making money and making things happen, and Jefferson Street became my mainstay.

You would never know it to look at Jefferson Street now, but at the height of its popularity, it had over 600 homes, businesses, and clubs. It was the only street in Nashville that we in the Black community could call "our street." It was exciting just to walk down Jefferson Street and see people cooking up soul food and barbeque in their front yards. Selling sandwiches and selling plates gave a lot of people who weren't in business a chance to make money on Jefferson Street. Others were able to help make ends meet for their families by selling water or cold drinks as people walked up and down the street.

There were so many clubs: The Tiki Lounge on 4th and Jefferson, Gants Club on 19th and Jefferson, The Flame Room, Hap Holidays Club, Brute Hayes Club, The Zanzibar Club, The Voters Club, Club Revalot, James Robertson's, Charlie Frierson's club, The Ebony Circle Lounge, and there was Pee Wee's on 51st, which was the white Pee Wee's, then the black Pee Wee's on 11th off Jefferson Street. These were just some of the other clubs that weren't as famous as the bigger clubs, but this shows how vibrant Jefferson Street was. There was endless entertainment going on over here on Jefferson and Centennial.

We had some other artists like Good Rocking Hoppy, Little Dynamite, Earl Gaines, Roscoe Shelton, Benny Latimore, Tyrone Smith, Jimmy Church, Watt Watson, Ironing Board Sam, Wig Walker, Gene Allison, Ted Jarrett, and Herman Young, who used to play saxophone at a club on Lafayette Street. Herman Young was a really good friend of mine. He used to have a boat, and we would go out on his boat a lot. Then we had Earl Gaines performing, and LC Scrubs, who still plays today. LC Scrubs is one of the premier musicians in the area and plays at Carol Ann's on Tuesday nights, at least before the pandemic hit. You could catch him out there, always sharp as a tack. LC also loves his jewelry, and he represents the culture – that's what I like about LC.

DeFord Bailey, Jr., a bass guitar player, was one of our local musicians who played with some big names such as Jimi Hendrix, who played in DeFord's backing band before he was famous. DeFord played back in the day at the big-name clubs – The Club Baron, the Del Morocco, Club Stealaway, and The New Era. He was also a regular on the TV show "Night Train." He was a really great guy.

The live music scene was supported by local disc jockeys who played the R&B tunes by the rising stars who brought crowds of fans to the Jefferson Street music venues. Independent labels sprang up with the help of radio play to sell their albums. "Night Train" was a popular television show that promoted Jefferson Street's talent.

So many of these musicians were top-notch, every bit as accomplished as the white musicians gaining popularity in the '50s and '60s. But only a few of Jefferson Street's favorites made it to stardom. Some came so close, like Cortelia Clark. He was a blind guitar player and a prolific songwriter.

I used to see Mr. Clark downtown in front of Woolworth's with his guitar. He had a little chair that he sat on while he played his guitar and sold shopping bags for 10 cents and 20 cents. We used to go downtown with my mother on some Saturdays and he would be there. They say he could tell when you'd drop a coin in his little metal cup when you'd take a bag, and he could tell you what coin it was – a dime, penny, nickel, or quarter. He could tell by the sound of it when it hit the cup.

Mr. Clark was a smart guy who came to Nashville from Chicago. He became blind after an operation at the age of 25. For many years, he worked in the broom factory, and that's where he met this other blind guy who taught him how to play the guitar. Mr. Clark could make up a song on the spot, just sitting there on that stool with his guitar, selling those shopping bags. He was well-known by all the Nashville regulars downtown.

There was this white kid, Mike Weesner, who used to come downtown with his grandmother when he was 9 or 10 years old. He always wanted to go by this spot where the blind guy would be singing the blues and selling shopping bags. His grandmother called the blues "devil's music." That's what they used to call the Blues because it was always sad music about somebody getting hurt, lovers breaking up, and people falling on hard times.

When Mike Weesner became a young man, he started his own production company. He would still go downtown and listen to Mr. Clark play his guitar. When he started his publishing company, he got Mr. Clark to agree to record some of his songs. Mike took the songs back to a friend of his, Felton Jarvis, who was a producer for Elvis Presley.

Elvis Presley had never gotten a Grammy or anything yet during that time. RCA recorded Mr. Clark's music and made an album of 10 songs called "Blues in the Street." They submitted it to the Grammy Association in 1966 and Mr. Clark got a Grammy for Best Folk Recording, beating out the group "Peter, Paul, and Mary," Ravi Shankar, Pete Seeger, and Leadbelly, who was a terrific blues singer.

I'm making this point because with all of this going on, Mr. Clark was in poverty at the time, lived on Jefferson Street, and then got picked up by Elvis Presley's producer, produced 10 tracks and won a Grammy for it. So why hasn't anybody heard about Mr. Clark, but everybody knows about Elvis Presley?

After Mr. Clark got the Grammy, RCA dropped him, because back then you could pass all of these white artists and get this Grammy, but you're still nobody. They just dropped him. They said he sold about 1,000 records, but he only got 3/4ths of a penny for royalties. So, he didn't make much money off of the music. He had to go back to selling his shopping bags and playing street music in order to survive.

In 1969, he lived right down here at 9th and Jefferson, right where the bicycle shop is now. It was a little frame house. He was filling his kerosene heater and the kerosene heater exploded and burned him. He went to the hospital, but when he got there, he couldn't eat anything, and he ended up dying after that fire. That was just another sad Jefferson Street story.

Muhammad Ali used to hang out on Jefferson Street and stayed at The Brown's Hotel a lot. One of the main reasons that he came to Nashville was because of Wilma Rudolph, the track star from Tennessee State who won 3 gold medals in the 1960 Olympics. Mohammed Ali kind of had a thing for Wilma Rudolph. While he was visiting, he hung out at the Del Morocco and The Club Baron, telling a lot of good stories about his boxing career, using his famous rhymes. Joe Louis, the boxer, and the great Jackie Robinson also used to hang out at the clubs and hotels on Jefferson Street.

There were many famous musicians who came through Nashville to play in the clubs on Jefferson Street on their way up the charts: B.B. King, Aretha Franklin, Etta James, Ray Charles, Miss Jackie Shane, and one of my favorites, Marvin Gaye. These famous Black musicians and artists and sports stars didn't have anywhere else where they could enjoy themselves and hear good entertainment when they came through Nashville, except on Jefferson Street.

Race was always a factor because they couldn't stay at the hotels, and they couldn't shop at the nicer stores and shops in the city. And they were world champions and famous musicians! But they could find everything they needed here on Jefferson Street. Brown's Dinner Club was one of the most prestigious clubs on Jefferson Street and the only club that was exclusive enough to have cloth napkins wrapped around the silverware.

In 1963, I met Samella Goodrum up on Jefferson Street. Back then, the college kids were all over Jefferson Street because there were three major historical black colleges right there: Fisk University, Tennessee State University, and

Meharry Medical College. Samella had finished Pearl High School, which was less than a half mile off of Jefferson Street. One night, Sam and her friends were going to Club Del Morocco to see Jimmy Hendrix before he became Jimi Hendrix.

Jimi Hendrix wasn't always the big star that he ended up being. He played in a number of bands around Nashville just to try to make money to survive. He played in Marion James' band and backed up a lot of the popular up-and-coming R&B singers, like Little Richard, DeFord Bailey Jr., and Joe Tex, along with many others.

They used to say, Music Row has country music, but Jefferson Street has Little Richard and Tutti Frutti. That was a big hit record and Little Richard was representing Tutti Frutti here on Jefferson Street. We were proud of that. After playing with Little Richard, Jimmy Hendrix had started making a name for himself as a headliner on Jefferson Street. But he hadn't changed the spelling of his name to Jimi yet. He was still Jimmy to all of us on Jefferson Street.

The night I met Samella, Jimmy hadn't come on stage yet, so she and her friends decided to go back up to the Stealaway, another famous Jefferson Street music club. It just so happened that I had visited friends at Tennessee State and was cruising back up Jefferson. I saw Samella and her friends standing outside in front of the Del Morocco looking for a ride back up Jefferson. Back then, all the women bummed rides. There wasn't all of that violence at that time, so you hardly ever heard of any incidents on Jefferson. I gave them a ride back up to the Stealaway.

That was an important ride, as it turned out. I got Samella's phone number. After that, we dated for close to three years before we actually got married in 1967. Then three years after that, along came our daughter, Tracey Michele Washington. That is one of my highlight memories of Jefferson Street – getting married to a lady I met on Jefferson Street and having a daughter who graduated from Tennessee State University with two degrees and still resides in Nashville, TN.

Chapter 5
Tragedy and Finding New Paths

In front of the Soul Shack in the '70s

A very sad event in our close-knit family happened in the early '70s that had a profound effect on all of us. Our brother Tink died in a car accident. He drove for a car dealership where he would go and pick cars up from Atlanta, Durham, and different places. I had that job at one time, and I gave that job to my brother. One night, he fell asleep and ran into a bridge. It broke his neck, killing him instantly. I was at my mother's house when the news came. That was a terrible time for my mother and for us. I saw more pain in my mother from that incident than I ever did before.

My brothers and I were all very close and even today, the three of us who are left get together regularly. My brother Seemore learned how to cook from our mother. All my grown life, he would brighten my day by dropping off some good food he would cook up on the weekends, even putting it in my refrigerator if I wasn't home. He would just come by and stack it up in my refrigerator. He still does that all the time, to this day. Staying in each other's lives and valuing these precious relationships was what our mother taught us. It was devastating to our family to lose Tink like that.

Peewee was always very attentive to our mother, watching out for her and paying most of the bills and staying with her. Even when she passed, we never had any problems or arguments over what my mother left behind to get divided up or distributed. I know some of my friends' families have had serious problems about how they were going to settle up the things that their parents left them, but that wasn't our way.

I began seriously pursuing my entrepreneurial ideas and started my own business in 1972, Lorenzo's Black and White Pig Pit Barbecue. I ran that from 1972 to 1974 on 15th and Buchanan Street in North Nashville. My brother Seemore was one of my best cooks at that place. We had two tables in the middle of the floor and a countertop around the wall for seating. I closed it down when so many other restaurants were opening around me, and people were only buying barbecue on weekends, especially black folk. We didn't eat a lot of barbecue during the week.

After I shut down the Barbecue pit, I started The Soul Shack Record Shop and Boutique on Buena Vista Pike. I sold records and different kinds of paraphernalia, leather goods, jewelry, and Black dolls. We also sold clothing made out of recycled denim. I had a few stars come by the record shop like Chaka Khan, members of the R&B group Sun, and Teddy Pendergrass.

When musicians were promoting their records, I had a really nice place for them to promote their music at my store. I entertained some of those artists and musicians coming through Nashville at the Soul Shack. Around that time, my son Dwayne had grown to be 14 or 15, and every now and then I'd look out the window and I'd see him riding his bike around in the parking lot. His parents lived in the community where my record shop was, and I kept my eye on him riding around the parking lot.

After a while, Dwayne finally came in and we got a chance to talk. I would only see him once every two or three weeks. Later, when he started college at MTSU and he needed a little financial help for school, he would come up to my house, and I would help him out. His mother and father didn't know at the time that he was coming up to see me. I did what I could for him during that period.

Shortly after that, in 1976, I started working with Moses Dillard and Jesse Boyce, two upcoming songwriter/producers in the Music Row area. They sought me out because they needed investors. I had some liquid cash at that point from all my entrepreneurial efforts. I went to Music Row with those guys and went into the music business as an investor and later, as a songwriting collaborator.

I kept the Soul Shack going until I was in the studio too much. It got to the point that we were in the studio all of the time. I had my cousin working the Soul Shack and he got kind of sickly on me. He would open up an hour late or later. We were supposed to open at 10 and he might open at 11 or 11:30. Finally, when I would go over there at 12 and he wasn't there, I couldn't continue like that, so I closed the Soul Shack and opened up another business on Mcferrin Avenue called The Game Room.

I brought some of the record stuff over there. I got my cousin, Bobby, to run The Game Room. I had three pool tables in there and about 15 pinball and game machines lined up around the walls. You could also buy records and jewelry in the front part. I kept that open for about a year. Then I just shut it down and put most of my energy into working with Dillard and Boyce and the music. I was doing all kinds of other things, but the music business was occupying more and more of my time.

That was a serious experience there, going to Music Row. We were the first Black production company to be accepted on Music Row. The "Production house" is where we wrote, produced, rehearsed, and trained new artists on Music Row. The "Production house" was a two-story brick house with beige carpet downstairs and brown carpet upstairs. There were two offices upstairs that were occupied by Jesse Boyce in one and me and Moses Dillard in the other.

A preproduction room was on the 2nd floor and a breakroom along with a lounge was downstairs on the 1st floor for guests. We ended up cutting five or six albums and collaborated with Peabo Bryson and Bobby Jones while on Music Row. We worked in all of the major studios on Music Row because we had budgets through Prelude Records out of New York.

One of the albums we cut over there, called Saturday Night Band, went to number 2 on the national disco charts. It was called a concept album – it wasn't by any one specific artist. Jesse Boyce did some songs, and so did Moses Dillard. Thomas Kain wrote some of the songs on the album, and I helped write a couple of them as well. Jackie Edmonds wrote a song on that album. The album went on to win two Grammy nominations.

By then, we were pretty busy traveling all around the country promoting the music. They were playing our music in Club 54 and all of the major clubs in New York City.

Prelude Records was promoting the albums in New York, and everybody thought the albums were being produced in New York. But they were completely produced in Nashville. Everything was about disco music at that point in time.

Music Row was a fun place to be back in those days because we were respected like "kings" in all of the major studios. Sound Stage Studio, Masterfonics, Pete Drake Recording Studio – we went to all of the major studios to record back in those days. Francis Preston with BMI welcomed Dillard and Boyce as disco producers, and BMI thought our team was going to break Nashville wide open. Here we came in with a different genre of music (disco) to Music Row, which is mainly Country Music, and it was being nominated for Grammys.

We were getting so much respect on Music Row, you wouldn't believe it. They called us Mr. This and Mr. That. Back in that time in the '70s, even with Black Power messages making it into mainstream media, it was still quite unusual for white men in Tennessee to address a Black man respectfully. It certainly wasn't something I was used to, growing up in Nashville.

At that point, disco music was being played all over the country. To be part of the history that Nashville was making by producing some of the best disco music out there was just amazing. That was a phenomenal thing. We had been on a couple of different TV shows, although I never was one of the big speakers on the shows. I had a briefcase just like everybody else. I was that silent person in the group, so they never knew what I was thinking. But there I was with these two major producers. Jesse Boyce, Moses Dillard, and me.

The I-40 expansion bridge over Jefferson Street

The City started planning for the Interstate 40 expansion in the early '50s. They started breaking ground in '63 or '64. But prior to that, there wasn't a whole lot being said to the community about the interruption of our neighborhood. The urban renewal powers-that-be had considered several routes for that expansion. Some of those routes would have torn up well-to-do white areas of Nashville, so those plans were quickly rejected. When the planners got busy with their red pens, the red lines ended up right on top of Jefferson Street.

This same scenario was being played out in urban areas across the country, seeking to break up Black neighborhoods and poorer neighborhoods under the guise of city "improvement" and often using the interstate highway system to do it.

In the early '60s, the Jefferson Street area had over 600 homes and businesses, paired with three HBCU (Historically Black Colleges and Universities) colleges. At that point, we had a variety of different levels of educated people. We also had the longtime local people on Jefferson Street, the political climate going on with the surge of the Civil Rights Movement, students marching, and the rise in popularity of many Black musicians.

The politicians, especially the white politicians, wanted Jefferson Street to go away because they felt our dynamic, exciting cultural center was too self-contained. The protests and marches going on for civil rights with all the Black students and activists in the area didn't exactly endear our neighborhood to the white leaders of Nashville, either. And they didn't like the attraction Jefferson Street's music scene held for young white music-lovers, some of whom were so determined to get into the Black-only venues that they put on darker makeup to try to get past the cops patrolling the streets.

We found out much later that notices about the public hearings that should have warned us about the I-40 expansion plans only appeared in white neighborhoods, and even those notices had the wrong dates for the hearings. So, the neighborhood only became aware of the City's plan to destroy Jefferson Street when it was too late. There was a hard-fought battle to save North Nashville from being torn apart, but the legal efforts ended in failure and the Interstate expansion took over.

By the early to mid-'70s, the expansion of I-40 was in full swing. The dust and construction traffic made it unpleasant as well as impossible for people to physically get to the clubs as massive bridges were built to carry the interstate through.

Street vendors were gone, clubs were closing, businesses were folding, and residents moved away as the interstate highway invaded Jefferson Street with its trucks, steel girders, and wrecking crews. It was heartbreaking to watch this happen. All the vibrant people out to enjoy each other's company, eat some great food, and hear wonderful music disappeared.

Gone were the clubs that had hosted big names, up-and-coming names, and started so many careers. Little Richard, B.B. King, Ike and Tina Turner, Jimi Hendrix, Etta James, Ray Charles, Aretha Franklin, Marvin Gaye, Otis Redding, James Brown, Jackie Shane, Earl Gaines, DeFord Bailey, Jr., Ted Jarrett, Marion James, Frank Howard, Jimmy Church, and so many others would never perform in those famous clubs on Jefferson Street again.

All of the interest in keeping Jefferson Street going began to dissolve when it became so hard for businesses to continue to grow. There was a lot of walking traffic from the colleges near Jefferson Street, but for those coming from other neighborhoods, the parking places began to disappear because there were 50 streets near and connecting to Jefferson Street that were torn up and turned into dead ends. Over 300 Black homes, businesses, and apartment buildings were destroyed at that time, along with several Black churches.

Maceo Thomas, the owner of Maceo's, was a local businessman who also had a roller-skating rink on the hardwood floor in the club space during the daytime for the teenagers, as did Club Baron. These places were popular gathering spaces for people of all ages. At night, from Thursdays through Sundays, there were always a lot of dice games, slot machines, and poker games going on, which helped keep people coming in, but there was less and less revenue to support music acts.

People who moved out of Jefferson Street just kept their heads up and tried to land on their feet somewhere else to make ends meet. The Black community lost its center, and there wasn't a place in any other Black neighborhood that could support the clubs and businesses to move.

The people with the money on Jefferson Street had gotten older and didn't invest back in the community, and very few of their families stepped up to reinvest to save Jefferson Street. E. W. Price's family stayed invested in the neighborhood. They ran Price's Dinner Club and invested in a clothing store, College Crib, for the fraternities at the nearby colleges. But for other investors in the community, it was too much of an uphill battle and a business risk to try to stay open.

During this time of decline, the colleges were still going strong, and the students were still eager to frequent the clubs. That was what kept the area fighting for its life through the '70s. There was no hope for the residents, however, because the Interstate forced them to move from their homes and businesses as real estate values dropped and buildings were torn down.

On top of all these setbacks, when segregation formally ended and Jim Crow left, Jefferson Street started really going down because Black folks could go to the white department stores, grocery stores, and hotels. Jefferson Street was no longer the only place where they could go. Once the property values started going down, and the City wasn't offering any help, the homeowners started moving out. Once they left, the businesses couldn't survive.

Jefferson Street was such a happening place, but eventually the traffic noise, dust, lack of parking, and frequent closing of various restaurants, bars, and clubs brought everything to a standstill. By the late '70s, every venue had closed, and the whole area looked like a ghost town. And that was that.

We could not maintain the precious musical and cultural heritage we had built. It was demoralizing to the community, and a great loss to the world of music. This decision made by the City of Nashville to sacrifice a thriving Black community was just one of many similar stories played out in the name of urban renewal and "progress" across the country in the 1970s.

As the bridges and roads took shape, cement was poured over the graveyard of failed businesses and lost livelihoods. And, as usual, a swarm of investors started to show up ready to snap up property at bargain prices and put up new buildings. Jefferson Street would become a newly gentrifying area close to the city, just like what happened in so many other American cities.

Chapter 7
Adversity and Grace

We came from poor neighborhoods, and however you could make a dollar, you tried. In the midst of the destruction of many of our livelihoods as the interstate construction moved in and the clear message that the City and the people in power did not want us to thrive and make money in our own community, times in the '70s became chaotic and restless, especially for younger Black people trying to make their way.

We didn't look upon selling a little marijuana or something as being a drug dealer. It was a hustle. As long as we wouldn't be hurting anybody or using a gun on them, we were doing all right. There were very few ways to get ahead for Black people, and in the late 1970s, more and more young people were turning to drug sales as a way to stay alive and get ahead.

Coming from an underprivileged family and community, I saw other people selling drugs and enjoying financial success, so I was adventurous and thought, let me try. So, in the midst of my other entrepreneurial efforts with the barbecue business and then the Soul Shack, I fell into the lure of "easy money" selling drugs as a side hustle. When I got a few years older, I decided to try it in another way using some of my connections in the music business. I got away with a lot of it at first. But in the end, you never get away. The odds always catch up with you.

In 1980, there came a big turning point in my life. In the midst of all the success we were experiencing on Music Row, I was drawn more deeply into some of the behind-the-scenes action in the growing use of drugs in the world of music and entertainment. I was arrested and accused of conspiracy to distribute drugs from Florida to Nashville. I was 37 years old.

Being so involved with the music business and with highly successful people, I had no intentions of informing on anybody. There were a lot of things taking place during that time that I had no control over. The things that I did have control of, I tried to do to my advantage. I had been fortunate to be around worldly people who traveled a lot and were very intelligent.

Though I didn't learn how to read until I was in my 20's and could barely read or write, I was smart, and I knew how to position myself with the right people. Since I knew how to do that, it put me where the money was. My thing was to try to get as much of it as I could while I had the chance, because the odds were always out there, and they were pretty heavily stacked against young Black men.

The night that I was arrested, I had taken some goods to a person's office on Music Row. When I got to the office, I knocked on the door a couple of times and the door flew open. Three or four officers stepped right up in my face and asked me what I had in the guitar case. By then there were probably 20 different officers surrounding me in that house – police, FBI, ICE officers, the DA – everybody was represented the night that I was arrested.

When I set the guitar case down, they asked me to open it. "I don't know what's in the case, sir," I said. "Could you open it?"

They got upset with that. A few of them looked me in the eyes and put their noses up to my nose. They were trying their best to intimidate me, cursing at me to open it up.

"Sir, you open it," I repeated. "I found this in a phone booth down the street and I just brought it here to get someone to check the guitar out."

Another officer walked up behind me and grabbed me by the shoulders. "Open up the guitar case," he shouted in my ear.

At that point they really started pushing me around. So, I reached down and opened up the guitar case. There was marijuana in the case, about 3 pounds. I had gone there to make a bigger deal than what was in the guitar case, but they had the evidence they needed. After that night, they wanted me to tell them where I got the marijuana. They had already found the cocaine that was in that building, but I didn't have cocaine with me.

They took me to jail and locked me up. I stayed in jail for 12 days while they tried to bring some other people into this thing, and they did. They brought some people in from Florida and had them all up here on a million-dollar bond. My bond was $100,000 and I had to pay my way out of that. I stayed in jail 12 days and then I got out on bond.

After that, I went to court. I went back and forth to court for three years, a total of 26 appearances. My attorney from that time is one of my best friends to this day. For some reason or another, someone stole my evidence out of the booking room at the police station. When I went to court for the 27th time, I was released because they didn't have the evidence. They had enough on me to give me probation, so I got five years' probation.

My judge for those 26 court appearances was the famous Judge A. A. Birch, who later went on to become the first African American Chief Justice of the Tennessee Supreme Court. They named a building after him, the A. A. Birch Criminal Justice Building in downtown Nashville. After seeing him that many times, I came to find out years later that he lived at an apartment complex behind the old

Howard School Building on Second Avenue. I ended up moving into that same building; it was a gated community.

Judge Birch didn't know me other than coming into his court all those times. I'm sure he thought that he was going to have to sentence me to something like 10 years in prison. That's what my lawyer had warned me was likely to happen. And I was prepared to do whatever time he gave me. But at the last minute, on my 27th court date, I was blessed, and I was saved.

During those three tense years, I had prayed to God that if he got me out of this, I would never, never touch another illegal substance for the rest of my life. He let me out of that, and that was the last time. I have never messed with illegal substances from that day to this day.

In 1983, I landed a job cleaning a car dealership, Thoroughbred Motorcars. Still today, I'm driving an Audi, and that's from the longevity of my relationship with that Audi dealership. The gentleman who hired me knew that I had been in all of that trouble, but he knew that I was trying to correct my mistakes. The owner gave me a contract to clean his dealership and trusted me, and I stayed with him for 26 years. The owner sold the dealership and recommended I stay as their vendor, so all in all, I've been with them for 38 years.

I'm still doing what I had promised God I would do, and that's work. When he gave me the job of owning a cleaning business, that was one of the best things that could have ever happened to me. God gave me a second chance, and here I am telling some of my stories about what took place when I was on the other side of the fence. That all ended in 1980.

During my five years of probation, I had to go to a class on a regular basis, and I had to pay a penalty fee every month. A couple of the probation officers I was under during that time said I was a model probationer, that I did everything right. I paid my money, I went to the classes, and I was never late. So, I didn't have any problems during those five years. The time went so fast, I didn't even realize my time was up. They had to call me and let me know that I was done.

Starting my own company was an exciting time in a way. It was challenging, but I fought and beat the challenge of going to jail. I didn't have any thought of doing any of the things that put me in that position again, because I knew God had stepped in and moved me from that scene to this one.

Chapter 8
Redemption, Boxing, and World Travel

With my best friend Morgan Hines of 40+ years

There was another blessing waiting in the wings for me during this time, this one from my best friend, Dr. Morgan Hines. Through him, I was able to enter the exciting world of professional boxing, and the road to that was one that we traveled together like brothers.

Morgan and I became friends in 1968. He's a New Yorker who came to Nashville to go to dental school in his 20s after college. I first met Morgan through one of his classmates, Terry Selman. Terry lived next door to me and had a party one night where I got to know Morgan. Terry, Morgan, and I became close friends – we called ourselves the Three Musketeers. Morgan's school, MeHarry Medical College, was right next to Jefferson Street where everything was happening. And the three of us stayed close through all the years since then.

We just lost Terry, our other Musketeer, recently. He went back home to Detroit and passed away there. As Morgan says, it makes you value your friendships even more when you lose a dear friend. It's so unusual to hear of people who have a true friendship after 50 years. Either one of us would give anything if the other person asked for it, and we've been that way all these years.

Instead of going back to New York after dental school, Morgan ended up going down to Columbia, TN, to go into business with a friend of his. After a couple years, he became a partner with this doctor and decided to stay in Columbia. He has his practice there to this day. I have not had to pay for any dental work for the last 45 years! Doc always takes care of me and won't take a dime. I couldn't force the money into his hands.

Morgan wanted to work with kids in his community, especially those from underprivileged communities who didn't have fathers at home, and he started a boxing club called the Columbia Tennessee Boxing Club. He said he wanted to give back, because so many men had helped him while he was growing up. We had a lot of time to work with these kids, train them, and change their mindset about a lot of things they were involved in down there in that small town. Many of these kids came and told us later how much of an impact we had on their lives.

Doc was down there by himself working with these kids and I saw that it was really taxing for him trying to keep things going and train these young fighters alone, so I started going down to Columbia two or three times a week to help him. He was mentoring some amateur young fighters to keep them off the streets and out of trouble. Sometimes we were successful at that, and sometimes we weren't. As the kids grew, he started taking some of them on the road to amateur competitions, and I went along as the other adult for these trips.

This experience was heartwarming on many levels. Seeing these boys turn into young men and knowing that they looked up to the two of us, especially Doc, as their father figures, was exciting and rewarding. We took them to Chattanooga, Memphis, Knoxville, and other small towns to enroll them in competitions. After a while, we began winning championships all over the South and Southeast, and I became a full-time/part-time trainer, as well as a friend and a "daddy" to some of the kids.

We started winning championships in the Golden Gloves competitions, which takes kids from one level to another in amateur boxing. We traveled to Colorado for the '94 Olympic trials while our guys were still amateur fighters. We had James Webb and Jamal Gardner who were in the

Olympic trials, and Webb was chosen to be an alternate on the Olympic team. Though he didn't end up going to the Olympics, it was quite a treat to have one of our fighters make it that far.

We ended up with several champion boxers from that boxing club, among them Sammy Sparkman, James "Spider" Webb, and Jerome Pillow. Sammy started with Morgan at around 8 years old. He grew up to fight pro all the way through 2009. Sammy was special, and he fought 41 professional fights, which is a lot more than most boxers fight. He was 14th or 15th in the world at one point. He is one of the nicest guys I've ever known, and we managed him throughout his career.

Boxing is not a kind sport, and fighters can get cheated out of things they should have won. For instance, if a promoter has your fighter on his card and doesn't want you to win, the judges will twist the results to make him lose.

My role was as a trainer and a "corner man." At most of these corners in the boxing ring, you would see three, four, or five people taking care of the fighter, because you only have 1 minute to do everything between rounds – to fix his cuts, cool him down, give him instructions, wipe up the corner, and get the stool in and out of the ring. Doc and I traveled together, and it was never more than the two of us in the corner.

I remember one fight we did in San Francisco. The fighter got cut over both of his eyes. Morgan had to work on one eye, and I had to work on the other while we cooled him down, gave him directions, then had to get that stool out of there and wipe down the corner. That's a lot to take care of in that one minute. After the fight, I was usually the one who took the fighters to the hospital to get sutured while Morgan stayed behind to finish up with the promoters. Morgan and I were a great team because we were such good friends.

Emanuel Steward, one of the greatest boxing trainers of all time, trained Sugar Ray Leonard and other famous boxers. We had the chance to match up against one of Steward's fighters, and it was strange because we felt like we had arrived. Morgan and I were in the corner at a televised fight with James Spider Webb against Emanuel Steward's champion José Celaya. Morgan went across the ring and told Emanuel Steward what an honor it was to fight against the greatest coach in boxing. We were so excited when we won that fight.

A little while after that big fight, James Spider Webb and Morgan Hines, as his trainer, were signed with the notorious Don King. I was the "second," who took care of fighters between rounds, so I wasn't signed, but Morgan had me come with them. I was part of his team. That was a big deal, being signed by Don King. After that, we traveled all over the world together to boxing tournaments and pro matches.

We ended up boxing for Don King for two or three years. At one point, James "Spider" Webb was rated number 11 in the world. This gave us a chance to travel all over Europe, Mexico, Puerto Rico, and about 35 or 40 cities in the United States. We did a lot of traveling during that time.

Kareem Abdul-Jabbar is Morgan's close friend from childhood, and when we went to Los Angeles for a fight with Spider, we all got to meet Kareem and went out to dinner. It was a tremendous night meeting such an elegant and reserved man who didn't let fame go to his head. We took pictures with him and the promoters, and he agreed to be in the photos even though he usually only agreed to be photographed with kids. We gave Kareem a front-row seat at the fight.

Then we experienced a big turning point in our forward momentum. We had the chance to box at Madison Square Garden on the night when Zab Judah was the main fighter at the top of the card. The boxing card shows several competitions taking place that night, and the person at the top of the card is the headliner. Judah was fighting for the world championship that night. I had the honor again of being the corner man for James Spider Webb that night in one of the opening fights before the headline matchup.

In the first round, Spider Webb had been beating his opponent ragged. The fighter he was fighting against had both eyes nearly closed from all the blows in the first round. This was in Morgan's hometown with all his friends there to watch. Spider was highly rated to win, and the crowd was on fire. Then Spider decided he was going to finish him off before the first round ended and somehow managed to run right into his opponent's desperate punch. Spider was knocked out, which was an unexpected shock to everyone.

That was a terrible loss for us. We were sick over it, literally. We had never lost like that before. We were in so much distress that we both walked away from the ring and threw up from all the tension and stress. A loss like that changes a boxer's career, and many boxers can't recover from it. Spider kept boxing, but it was the beginning of the end for him and a big setback for all of us.

After we left Don King's empire, we went to a championship fight in Poland for the light-middleweight title there. They treated us really well. Sammy Sparkman fought the Polish fighter and at the end of the fight, the audience gave Sammy a standing ovation. The judges didn't award him the fight, but the crowd loved his performance and disagreed with the outcome. Sometimes it just goes that way with the judges. When you are fighting your way up in the system without a famous promoter behind you, you can work your heart out and not get the wins.

It was interesting to be in a country where there were no Black people. People would point at us as if we were from another planet. But they treated us respectfully and generously in Poland. Just to walk inside those buildings with all the old European history of a palace converted to a fighting arena is so different from the arenas we have here in the States. Renovating an ancient building like a palace sounds amazing, but we preferred the newer arena buildings in the States.

On one of those trips, we met a female fighter from Italy, Francesca Lupo. She wanted to continue her boxing career in America. She couldn't speak English and Morgan couldn't speak Italian, but we managed to train her and find her a place to stay. She was the toughest woman we have ever known. She would get in the ring with the men and box like a man. They respected her. She would say, "I'm Sicilian woman!"

We prepared her for a female world championship in England at Leeds Arena near London. She didn't become a champion, but she was a great fighter and put on a great show. At the end of the show, the promoter kept stalling about paying us, which was unusual in the professional circuits. That was our first time in London. There was a highly respected Englishman there who was a member of some prestigious club, and he saw that we were having a problem getting paid. He went to the promoter and said if he didn't pay us, he was going to ruin his reputation using his connections at the newspaper. So, we finally got paid.

This nice Englishman took us all around London, to the bunker where Winston Churchill was during WWII, the Tower of London, Westminster Abbey, and the different royal family residences, the changing of the guard, and all those tourist attractions. It's always great to have someone who lives there to take you around, and it was a wonderful time.

We also fought at Caesar's Palace in Vegas, and at the MGM Grand in Vegas. We had Sammy Sparkman in one of the warmup fights for the crowd before the big fight. That night at the MGM Grand was called The Fight of the Century, with Oscar de la Hoya and Sugar Shane Mosley. All these celebrities were there, and the place was packed.

We had another fight in Washington, DC, with Sammy Sparkman where we got a chance to meet many older world champions – Lennox Lewis, Floyd Mayweather, Larry Holmes, Gerry Cooney, Joe Frazier, the Spinks brothers, and Ken Norton. It was our chance to sit down and talk with these great boxers, and it was mind-blowing. Most of those men are gone now, and it was great to be there with Morgan to enjoy that experience together.

Chapter 9
Big Changes and More Ventures

With my children: Dwayne, Tracey, Pat, and Ryan

The boxing trips went all the way through 2006 with Morgan, but during that same time, there was also a lot going on for me in Nashville in the years following my Divine rescue from being sent to prison. I moved to 2000 8th Avenue South in 1983. I lived in apartment D and ran my office from there when my cleaning business, Lo's General Cleaning, was starting up.

Cynthia Purham lived in apartment B. I would see her every day when she came down the steps going to her car. I introduced myself at last, we got to be really good friends, and we started dating. She was a very attractive lady, and very smart. I really liked intelligent women. It made up for some of my underprivilege. We moved out of that building and moved in together. Our son, Ryan, was born in 1988, and though Cynthia and I never married, from that point until now, we have been good friends.

There were other big changes at all levels of my life while I was fulfilling my 5 years of probation. I felt like my past was being brought up to me in a new light, and there were new beginnings and understandings in store for me. When I first got busted in 1980, I had prayed to God. That was one of my big changes. I'll never forget the despair of being held in jail 12 days, with no one allowed to visit me or anything. I was so down and depressed and I asked God to get me out of this. I didn't want to go to prison. If he would get me out of this one, I said I would never do anything else illegal, or anything to disgrace His love for me.

After I was let go from jail and court with only 5 years probation to serve, all the businesses I started were legal. I did not go back to those crimes again that got me arrested. I truly believed that I was going to have to serve at least 10 years, since my crime carried a sentence of 10 years to life. After that, I was deeply grateful to God for releasing me from the nightmare of a long prison term. Around the time my probation ended, I decided it was time to completely change my life. I joined a church and committed my life to God. It was at Mount Bethel Baptist Church.

I wanted God to really keep his hand on me and keep me away from all of the criminal ideas and thoughts that I had. And those thoughts did come up at times, because I was so connected with smart people. I could always brainstorm ideas and find people to join up with me to do the things I wanted done. I could convince very intelligent people to make me a part of what they were doing. That was one of my skills. My skills weren't the books, my skills were dealing with people.

Once I joined the church, opportunities arose to reconnect with the children I had lost due to my lifestyle choices in my younger years. I hadn't really talked with my first child, Pat, until she was in her 30s. When I was in church, John, her father, was a deacon, and I was president of the usher board. One Sunday we had men's day. John had invited all of his kids to come to church,
and Pat came.

When she was born, she didn't look anything like her dad and his family, and nobody ever talked about whether or not she was his daughter or somebody else's daughter. Back then, a child who came into your house was your child. She and I had never talked about her being my daughter and not John's daughter.

That Sunday, John came down from the pulpit and walked toward the back of the church where I was standing at the door as an usher. When he came down that aisle, I could sense something in him because I had been telling myself that we needed to settle this right here. Here we were, both Christians. I was an usher president and he was a deacon coming up, and a bright young man. I was thinking, 'Well today, I'm gonna deal with this lie that we've been living for 30-something years. It's not going to go any longer than this.'

Right after I had those thoughts, it was as if he was up there at that pulpit listening to me thinking to myself. So, he walked down that aisle, walked up to me, put his hand out, and we shook hands. It was like we locked hands for what seemed like 30 minutes, but it couldn't have been more than a minute. In this handshake, there was a conversation. Without saying a word, I felt we were both saying, 'Let's leave it alone. Let's leave it where it is.'

Then he turned around and walked back up to the pulpit and I went outside the doorway. A few minutes after that, Pat came up to me and shook my hand. She handed me a note with her phone number in it. A couple of days later, I gave her a call. She let me know her thoughts and feelings about how she thought our relationship should be. Her aunt had told her about me when she was 12 years old. So, she had already known, all this time, which was a surprise to me.

Pat's birthday is the same day as mine. She told me that her parents had been great to her, and her stepdad treated her just as well as he did any of the other kids, and she didn't want to hurt either one of them. She said, as long as we both knew, that's the way she wanted to keep it, and I was in agreement with it. For me, it was like closing a great void from my early years. It took away some of the guilt I experienced, and I felt that I was giving her a part of her life that she considered as lost. It was a difficult situation living that lie for so many years. I was glad that it ended that Sunday at church because it was also tearing me apart.

Right around that same time, my son Dwayne, who had been in and out of my life only sporadically, actually came to me and started working for me. I made him a supervisor on one of the cleaning teams that I had. Within a very short time, he was all over it, taking charge of details and stepping up to manage the day-to-day demands of running the business. He was making me semi-retired; I hardly had to go to work at all. Dwayne was taking care of everything. He is a smart guy and very energetic.

After a while, Dwayne moved on to take another job and started a church. He stopped working with the cleaning service and devoted most of his time to his ministry. Today, I'm a member of his church. Dwayne and I have a great father/son relationship. When his stepfather was living,

Dwayne would also say he was very fortunate because he had two fathers. I also have a close relationship with all of Dwayne's children and grandchildren.

So, during that period of time in the 1980s, a lot of healing was taking place in my family and especially between me and my children. I was looking around, like I always do, for more opportunities to build wealth for all of us.

I had been working with a chemist friend and his team to develop a windshield washer cleaner for trucks and planes that could handle the problems caused by bugs on the windshield. I knew some people who had a couple of small planes, and they complained about the difficulty of getting the dead bugs off the windshield so they could see. The product we were working on would soften the dried-on bugs and allow windshield wipers to push the bugs right off the windshield. The chemists came up with a couple of great ideas for the airplanes and the tractors and trailers, but the alcohol scent was so strong that we were afraid it would put the drivers to sleep after spraying the windshield washer on the windows. So, we had to abandon that invention.

Then, another opportunity for a new venture arrived. I had two friends who owned a McDonald's restaurant, and they had two friends, one in Chicago and one in Detroit. Among the four friends, they owned a total of about 14 McDonald's restaurants. They were all entrepreneurs. They wanted to present a hand soap to the McDonald's franchise. And I already had my chemist friend with a brother who was a really sharp young businessman. So, I thought, if I could pull all these people together and we came up with this soap, we could very well become millionaires, because the soap would be distributed to all of the McDonald's around the world.

Once all the players were introduced and the ideas started to flow, things moved along quickly. We were going to build a manufacturing plant. We had the property and the building to set the plant up in, over on 5th Avenue near Monroe. We had everything that we needed to develop the soap and distribute it to McDonald's. I was paying for all of the chemicals, flowers, oils, and other supplies we needed to make the soap. That was my thing, to pay for all of that and watch over the soap being developed.

It took about 8 months, but we ended up with a soap that McDonald's agreed to purchase. Then we planned a meeting for the two brothers who owned the McDonald's here in the Nashville area with the chemist and his brother. But the head chemist was about 30 minutes late. He had stopped off at a bar for a couple of drinks before the meeting. Before he got to the meeting, the McDonald's owners had laid a $700,000 check on the table. The check was to set the warehouse up, to develop the soap, buy a couple of trucks, and get ready for distribution.

So, in struts the chemist, late and with alcohol on his breath. He demanded some ridiculous things at that meeting. He wanted a boat. He wanted to go to the Bahamas. He wanted a month's vacation, and a stack of cash to support the trip. The investors said, "Okay, now, we are coming together in a partnership, and we see how in 2 or 3 years we all can be very, very wealthy. But you're asking for all of these luxuries for you personally, right now? So, what we will do here is we will dissolve this meeting."

By that time, we had been there for two or three hours already, but when we got to the final part of the meeting, that was the end of it.

"We are going to pick the cashier's check up off the table. If we have these kinds of problems with this guy now, I can just imagine how it could escalate later," one of the McDonald's owners said.

And they canceled out that deal. I had spent around $1,000 already on supplies. These investors used to bring food over to my office from their McDonald's for our lunch, just so we had some things to snack on while we all worked together to develop the soap. Up to that meeting, everything seemed like it was going to go smoothly, but then it all went wrong just like that. The participants in this enterprise are still around here in Nashville, and we all should be very wealthy people right now, but one guy's attitude spoiled the whole effort.

I felt like that was the one big break that I definitely could have seen through, supplying soap to McDonald's all over the world. It was just like everything I have become involved with in my life. I didn't know anything about operating a restaurant or running a record store, just like I didn't know anything about developing soap. But I had people around me who said they could do it, so I invested in them and their ability to produce.

It was the same way with the music with Moses Dillard and Jesse Boyce. I wasn't a record producer or a publisher, I couldn't write songs – I didn't do any of that. But I teamed up with some guys that I felt that I could support and be a part of in this big music scene. We were supposed to be the hottest thing in Nashville. We thought we were going to be as big as country music. But Disco music went out as fast as it came in. That's when Hip-Hop came into play. Hip-Hop pushed Disco out.

A few years later, as I was continuing to build my cleaning business, an old friendship from Jefferson Street rekindled when Barbara Washington reentered my life. She was a special part of different portions of my life. I met her originally in 1972 while she was walking down Jefferson Street on her way to Tennessee State. We became friends at that point. She went on to finish Tennessee State and moved to Atlanta. After 20 years, a friend of ours had spoken with her and then got in touch with me. Barbara and I exchanged phone numbers again, and she moved to Nashville. Shortly after that, in 1993, we got married. We stayed together for about 15 years until we separated. We are still good friends.

Barbara and I started Office Transformation Systems together. In addition to offering cleaning services, OTS was a bookkeeping and business support company helping businesses switch their offices over to computers. On the cleaning services side, I was hiring men from the Nashville Union Mission. I worked with over 200 guys from the rescue mission. I was giving these men jobs when they couldn't find employment anywhere else. I did that for about 20 years. The majority of the employees I hired came from the mission, so I was able to help a lot of ex-soldiers, military people, and survivors from the criminal justice system.

Many of these men traveled from one city to another just for survival. I understood those guys and their problems. We would talk and pray together, eat together, and work together. They were a big part of the success that I had with the cleaning business for a number of years. Quite a few of those guys have passed on since then. A lot of them were in transition, going from one city to another and staying at missions in different cities. They might be at the Union Mission in Nashville this week, then 3 weeks later, they could be in the Union Mission in Detroit. The mission provided them bus passes to go from one city to another.

I heard one guy say that being at the mission was like being a part of a poor man's country club because they could eat, bathe, and get free clothes. Some of them were serious about getting out of the mission. One of them came to work with me regularly, left the mission, and was with me for about 10 years. He didn't go back to the Union Mission. He ended up going back home to North Carolina. One of the guys who worked with me a lot back then died about three months ago. He was a really good friend and he stayed in touch, but he lived out his life at the Union Mission.

A lot of them had drug problems and people would ask me why I would want to hire those guys from down at the mission knowing all the problems they carried with them. I would tell them that at one time, I was just about to become one of those guys. As long as the men respected me and my jobs, I would respect them and give them a chance. And I did. I only had one guy steal from me out of the 200 guys who worked for me over the years. But I knew who it was who had taken a 100-dollar bill and a pistol from one of my clients during a cleaning. Even though that employee gave it right back to me and I returned the stolen goods to the client, they still fired our company from the project.

When Barbara and I dissolved OTS, I launched Clean Tech, which is the cleaning business I still own and operate now.

Chapter 10
Back to Music, Back to Jefferson Street

**Herbert "Salwafare" Turner,
Outta Da Box Artist**

In 2000, I had been out of the music business for years and had kept myself busy with the cleaning service and other entrepreneurial ventures. I was almost semi-retired, because I wasn't going out to a lot of the jobs myself anymore, and all I had to do was manage the teams. Jesse Boyce came to me and wanted to know if I would come over to 12th Avenue and start another studio with him, Dion Brown, and Anthony Graves. They had some artists they wanted to produce, and they had the building and most of the equipment already set.

I thought about it and after a good meeting with them, I decided to go back into the recording business for their studio, Outta Da Box. We worked together on that for a couple of years. We were down on 12th Avenue South near Music Row, right there where they built the police station.

Herbert "Salwafare" Turner was our first Hip Hop artist. He was an ambitious young artist, and we latched onto that energy. He was a good rapper and also a good producer. He was very talented at influencing and directing other artists. We cut an album for him and he worked with us on albums for other artists as well. I wish we would have had more resources to promote his music. Shanté was a female rapper who was also a part of the Outta Da Box family, and so was a group called 4Sale.

The building we were in was so expensive to rent, and on top of that, the place was broken into a couple of times. The studio lost keyboards, instruments, and recording equipment from those break-ins. After about two years, we closed that place down. We moved to another location and started another record label up on Music Row called Brighter Day Records. So, part of our effort was for Hip Hop, and the other part was for Brighter Day Records, a gospel music label.

Jesse Boyce had become a minister, and that's where a lot of the gospel music came in. Anthony Graves and I were doing the Hip Hop music, and Jesse wanted to be more involved with gospel because he wanted to remove himself from the Hip Hop genre. Jesse brought in a couple of really great gospel musicians, a keyboardist and a guitarist. And of course, Jesse had played bass guitar for Little Richard for about 20 years, so I got a chance to see Little Richard and be involved with that set, too. Jesse brought a whole world of music experience as a veteran of so many great bands.

The Hip Hop that we took to Music Row worked out well for a couple of years, but then it got to be so expensive. I was taking care of a lot of the expenses during that time hoping we could get that hit record. As usual, I was investing in the talent and intelligence of other people, because I believed they could make things happen.

When we were producing Hip Hop music, there was a lot of profanity in it. I kept trying to tell these guys, "Okay, you cut the profanity out of it so that we can take this music to the mainstream," because it was good enough. But the rap artists felt that the trend was to use this kind of language in the music. They refused to change that way of thinking or change their style of writing. I was trying to get them to go from profanity to just using good common-sense language in order to make money. You can make more money getting yourself played on the radio than you could going underground.

So, I had problems with the guys from that perspective. After a while, we closed the studio up on Music Row. It was a good address, but it was very expensive. So, we left Music Row, and I put a small studio in the back room of my office on 8th Avenue. I went in and reconstructed the whole bathroom and the office, making it all soundproof. We started recording a couple of the young artists.

A lot of people thought we were going to be in the rap business because of the players that we had around us. We had all of the components that we needed, right there in-house. We had producers, engineers, and musicians. The whole package was there, but we could not become successful. One of the reasons for that was because we didn't have the inside connection to the bigger record labels.

If you don't have a major label pushing you, it's really hard. They tell you about selling music out of your trunk until you make it. That might take 10 or 15 years. It did take some of those guys that long to make it by producing and marketing themselves. It can be done, but it takes a lot of time and effort and money, even to produce yourself.

In 2010, we moved to our current location on Jefferson Street and changed the name of the label to Out Da Box Entertainment. We stopped producing Hip Hop music and focused on Christian music, jazz, and R&B. Don Adams was one of the most talented bass players to come from New Jersey to Nashville, and his was the first jazz album we produced at Out Da Box. Don helped a number of the artists and musicians promote their talents by inviting them to be in his band. His band played around the community and out-of-town gigs. Don Adams is a very talented songwriter and arranger, still playing gigs, and very popular.

A friend of mine for over 20 years is Richard Manson, an attorney. I had been working with Richard to help me manage the legal side of running the cleaning service. When I got to the point of moving my studio to Jefferson Street, I went to Richard's office in Brentwood and sat down with him. I wanted to talk about building the recording studio and the record label. That was my big thing at the time. I wanted to do what Barry Gordy did in Detroit. We had all of these artists and musicians here in Nashville that weren't doing anything major. I also met with Don Adams and said, "Man, do you think we could pull a band together like Barry Gordy did in Motown, and then bring some of these young artists and musicians up and take them into the studio and record them? See if we could find them a deal somewhere?" I didn't know how tough it was to find them a deal! That's major, getting with some record company and getting them to listen to your artist.

That was how I got the new studio on Jefferson Street started, and then Richard Manson encouraged me. He said,

"Okay, Lorenzo, if you're gonna come to Jefferson Street, you gotta do some things on Jefferson Street. First, you need a song about Jefferson Street." I had to think about that for a while.

It was when I moved back to Jefferson Street that all the memories of the music, the people, the businesses, and the families came flooding back to me. Being in the world of music again brought me back in connection with many of the fine musicians from the past. Many of them were still around doing good work and keeping the legacy alive the best they could.

Jefferson Street had been such a vibrant center of our lives. But the entertainers knew how vibrant it was because they had been a part of the excitement that took place over there back in the day. I began feeling a growing desire to do something to help preserve all the old stories, photographs, and accomplishments – all the precious history that had been made on Jefferson Street.

My biggest inspiration to get all of it going at first was Marion James, Nashville's Queen of the Blues, and also Jesse Boyce. Marion James had started the Musician's Aid Society. The Musician's Aid Society assisted artists and musicians that were down on their luck. Marion sometimes would cook a big pot of chili or stew and invite some of the artists to come by and eat, the ones who were having a tough time.

She had been doing that for musicians for as long as I could remember. Even Jimmy Hendrix went by Marion James's place and had stew or chili or a good meal at her house.

So, Marion was a motivating source when it came to encouraging the artists and the musicians who played on Jefferson Street. Marion James' husband, James "Buzzard" Stewart, was a saxophone player and one of the best horn arrangers to come through Nashville. He worked with the Muscle Shoals Horns. That was a popular set of horn players, with Harrison Calloway and those guys. James used to let the horn players sleep on his floor when they would come up to do some arrangements from Muscle Shoals, AL.

So, Marion and I became good friends at that point. I asked, "Marion, we need a song about Jefferson Street."

Marion said, "Oh yeah? I already got it."

"You already got it?" I was amazed. She had already written a song called "Back in the Day" about the nightclubs and the people who played in the clubs, singing about Jefferson Street. That song was perfect. I just wish we had been able to put a little better spin on it. Don was trying to take it on as jazz and Marion James was a blues singer, so that was a conflict of styles, but it turned out pretty well.

There was nobody else giving Jefferson Street the attention, devotion, and notoriety it deserved. So, I decided I wanted to help bring the fame back to Jefferson Street. Nobody was talking about the artists and musicians who played here. Every now and then somebody would mention Jimi Hendrix and how he got his start here in Nashville on Jefferson Street.

Billy Cox is another amazing Nashville musician whose career was connected with Jimi's, but no one was mentioning his name. Billy met Jimi when they were both in the Army at Fort Campbell, Kentucky, and they started jamming together. Then Billy became Jimi's first bass player right before Jimi Hendrix became an international sensation. He played with Jimi again later in his career.

Billy told me he felt that nobody in Nashville was giving him recognition or credit for all that he did for the music here. So, I had a wonderful mural of Billy and Jimi Hendrix put on my wall on the outside of the building, painted by Nashville visual artist LaRhonda Angelisa. This was just one of the things I did to call attention to the powerful legacies we have here.

Some of the great musicians who were still going strong in Nashville included Clifford Curry, who sang on the famous TV show, American Bandstand, and had several hit songs including "She Shot a Hole in My Soul." Another Jefferson Street veteran I met around 2011 through Marion James was Lucius Talley. He is a drummer who also played spoons and was a part of Marion's organization, the Musician's Aid Society. Recently, he has been going around the city to teach schoolkids how to play spoons through the National Museum of African American Music's educational programs.

Another great jazz bass player, Watt Watson, also played bass on Etta James' hit record "Rock the House." His band was one of the first bands to play at Brown's Dinner Club for famous visitors like Jackie Robinson, BB King, Joe Lewis, Ella Fitzgerald, Nat King Cole, Aretha Franklin, and others.

Levert Allison is Gene Allison's brother. Gene Allison was a great singer and had the first hit coming out of Jefferson Street called "You Can Make It if You Try" in the early 1960s. Levert, also a great singer, used to stand in for his brother when Gene couldn't make the gig. Now, Levert sings with the Fairfield Four, who recently received another Grammy award. His group has sung in many famous places, including the White House.

It was impossible to be around all these famous local and national musicians and not want to do something special to keep all those legacies alive somehow.

Chapter 11
The Birth of the Jefferson Street Sound Museum

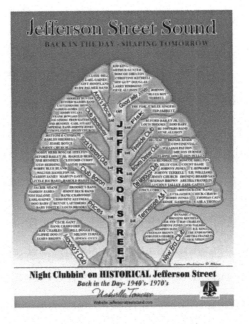

**Jefferson Street Sound Tree showing all
the clubs and artists on Jefferson Street
from the 1940s to the 1970s**

I began hanging pictures up in the front room of the studio there on Jefferson Street before I ever thought to turn it into a museum. I invited different artists over in the beginning, so it wasn't the public coming into the studio space. It was mostly just folks who had something to do with entertainment. A lot of the artists and musicians who were still here with us were concerned about Jefferson Street losing the prestige it had built over the years when they were playing there. They were also afraid that their legacies were going to be lost.

Since these older artists were good friends of mine, I decided that I would do something to help them preserve their legacies. I started collecting more pictures, shoes, pins, whatever I could get from the artists who were still here with us, then I displayed my collections in that front room of the Jefferson Street Sound studio. That's when I started this museum, the Jefferson Street Sound Museum.

Folks started telling me that I had the first Black museum here in Nashville. And I said, "This is not just a museum. It's a community resource. It represents the community and it's here for the community."

It started out just for people actually from the community, especially the ones who had played in these clubs and played with some of the bigger acts like Jimi Hendrix and Ray Charles. A lot of these local musicians made it to fame too, right here in Nashville, and then many of them became national and international stars. Jefferson Street was a stepping stone for so many talented people, and I wanted to honor their lives.

Marion James had kept a lot of the artists and musicians in Nashville motivated and together through her Musician's Aid Society, and she was a bright light to all of us. We became very close during the last years of her life. When she was in a nursing home or the hospital, I took her dinner every Sunday and we'd watch football games together. She came up with a song idea one Sunday. "Lorenzo," she said, "I just thought of a song title: Football ain't no woman, but it sure can take your man."

She never got the chance to record that idea, but I'm working with my old friend Thomas Cain, who is known around town as a songwriter and musician, to put that line to music, record it, and get it out to the public. The Musician's Aid Society is still going on, even after Marion passed away in December of 2015. I'm the treasurer of that organization today. She played a big role in getting the museum idea off the ground, and I owe her a debt of gratitude.

I hosted a dinner at the museum in 2012. I invited some of the old musicians – Marion James, Jesse Boyce, DeFord Bailey, Clifford Curry, Frank Howard, Nick Nixon, Tyrone Smith, Lucius Talley, and Jimmy Church – they were all still with us at the time. So, I had all of these great musicians who gave their lives to entertainment. We talked about what it was like to perform on Jefferson Street. It was more than just going and doing a gig. To them, it was like, "I'm going to make a bunch of people happy tonight because I'm going to put on a great show. One of the best shows that I've ever done, I'm going to do that tonight."

That was the attitude of a lot of the musicians and artists who played on Jefferson Street, whether they made it to stardom or not. They had pride in creating great music for their community. As I started putting their names on paper, I worked with my friend Morgan Hines to create the Jefferson Street tree that you see pictured at the beginning of this chapter. I put the names of a lot of those artists and musicians who played in the clubs on that tree that we designed.

The limbs on the tree represent the night clubs and the learning institutions that were on Jefferson Street during the '40s, '50s, and '60s. The leaves on the tree represent the artists and musicians who actually played in those clubs. I hope that tree will go down in history to remind future generations of these incredibly talented people who played on Jefferson Street, the ones who did and the ones who didn't make it big.

With Marion's encouragement, I added more items and photos to my collection. There is an oil painting of Marion in the entryway, an evening gown of hers in the corner, a bass strap from Billy Cox in a glass case, a spoon from Lucius "Spoonman" Talley, and a personalized guitar from Jesse Boyce, to mention just a few of the many memorable artifacts. There are photos of Ironing Board Sam, Clifford Curry, Little Richard, and many, many other Jefferson Street artists lining the walls.

As the collections grew, I started opening up and inviting teachers to bring their kids by to see what I had on the walls and to hear some of my stories about the artists and musicians who played here on Jefferson Street. I wanted the children to know about these entertainers who had so much pride in what they had done, and in what they were still doing, and I made sure to invite them to speak at the museum with the kids, also. Their stories of Jefferson Street during the late 50's through the early 70's were an inspiration to everyone.

I once had a group of about 23 young people come in. The two adults who brought these young people to the museum were looking at a board I made showing the fallen stars, the artists and musicians who had passed on. One of the adults saw the picture there of Jackie Shane, the famous transgender singer and drummer who got her start in Nashville before she left the South for Canada to continue her career.

In the 1950s, she was one of the first and bravest public entertainers to take the stage being a trans woman in Nashville or anywhere. The people in the South were not only cruel to Black people but especially cruel to a Black trans woman. The guy who was looking at the picture of Jackie in the museum turned to me and said, "No, Jackie Shane isn't deceased. Everyone thought she died in

California. She doesn't want people bothering her, but she lives right here in North Nashville in Germantown."

I said, "What?!" I asked him to give Jackie Shane my number. She didn't call me for two weeks because she was a recluse. She didn't talk to people because so many were nasty and cold. When Jackie called me, we talked for over 2 hours on the phone. We had all of this history in common. Everything I was trying to represent in the museum was our shared memory.

I invited her into the museum and showed her the picture I had put of her with the fallen stars. We took a picture together in front of that memoriam wall. This is the only known picture of Jackie Shane taken in 45 years. Unfortunately, she passed away before she could take any other pictures. Just before her death, people were talking about making a documentary about her in Toronto, Canada.

Jackie had some bad memories of Toronto. A lot of musicians, especially African American musicians, did not get their due pay from the record labels back in those days. The labels owned the rights to almost all of the songs. Most of the musicians, including Jackie Shane, died broke. This is a story that has been repeated over and over again through the years of Jim Crow and after. People need to be aware of these ways in which Black artists have been taken advantage of. Despite their great talent and fame, too many did not receive the money they should have.

After all the music she released and the many fans she had in Canada, there should have been royalties that would have kept her comfortable in her retirement. These days, her recordings are so hard to find that people are paying hundreds of dollars for her old single records.

Her family is still trying to get money for her releases to this day.

Jackie accepted me as part of her family when she found out how I supported Marion James, and she wanted that, too, she told me. I respected Jackie for who she was – a very sophisticated person, knowledgeable and intelligent. She shared some of her stories from her years in Canada, how she met club owners and the respect that she got while she was in Canada that she didn't get here in the U.S. She felt very threatened here, which is one of the reasons she went to Canada. She heard it was so much better over in Canada when it came to gender differences as well as race.

She played regularly with Frank Motley, a very popular trumpeter and bandleader. Then Jackie traveled between Toronto, Los Angeles, and back to us in Nashville to appear on our popular local TV music show Night Train. She moved on from playing with Frank Motley after a while and kept gigging in the '70s in LA, Las Vegas, Toronto, and Nashville.

She was even approached to join forces with George Clinton's music collective Parliament-Funkadelic, but she turned that down.

Jackie told me that she felt so good being in Canada that she stayed for a number of years. As a young man, she had felt she was a woman trapped in a man's body. She told me how heartbreaking that was when she was coming up. Her mother and her grandmother accepted her for who she was. There were other family members who did not accept her, though. I have so much admiration for this person who had such respect for life, for herself, and for others.

Jackie said, "Lorenzo, I just want to live and let live. I don't want to complicate anyone else's life, and I don't want anyone to complicate mine." She was just that kind of person. She felt dearly for me because I genuinely respected her and her lifestyle and her way. That was the way my mother and grandmother taught me, to accept people for who they are, which I learned from an early age.

Jackie's story is just one of many, many stories I share at the museum. I also tell the story of my old childhood friend Herbert Hunter and his friendship with Ted Jarrett, considered by many to be a giant of Nashville R&B. Herbert was always a singer from 5 or 6 years old. I remember they would stand him up to perform in front of everyone at Christmas time and picnics. By the time Herbert turned 16, with me in tow, he started getting noticed singing R&B on Jefferson Street.

In the 50s, Ted Jarrett was already getting well-known as a songwriter, producer, and radio dee-jay on the famous African American R&B station, WSOK. In 1955, his record "It's Love, Baby (24 Hours a Day)" hit Number 2 on the Billboard chart with Nashville's young R&B star Earl Gaines singing. Then he hit the top 5 again in 1957 with "You Can Make It If You Try," with a great vocal by Gene Allison.

So, by the time Herbert, with me in tow, started singing on Jefferson Street, Ted Jarrett was an established R&B powerhouse. There was a little restaurant that Ted used to eat lunch at pretty much daily back then. He could get the lunch cheap, and the place had a really good cook, just like most of the restaurants on Jefferson Street. Ted used to go into this little restaurant, and he would play the jukebox while he was in there having lunch.

Herbert would stand outside the door of the restaurant and sing to the jukebox music, hoping to attract Ted's attention. One day, Ted walked out the door and asked Herbert who he was. And that was the beginning of their friendship. Ted took Herbert over to his mother's house and introduced him to his mother. His mother really liked Herbert. She had an extra room in her house, and she treated Herbert like her own son, inviting him to stay with her.

In the meantime, Ted was taking Herbert to his office over on Jefferson Street and into the studio. Ted got a pretty good record out of that. Back then, they were just recording 45's. One of them got on the radio. It was a really big song called "Isn't It Wonderful to Dream," and Herbert bought himself a brand new '61 Ford Galaxie convertible. That was a big deal. I would drive that car for Herbert so he could sleep after being up all night singing in the clubs.

Ted never learned how to drive, so he also got me to run him around town to different artists' houses, the studio, anywhere he needed to go. I was always driving him somewhere. Herbert used to do that, but once Herbert got busier, I took on the job of driving Ted around. Ted was just a great, great guy. Everyone was crazy about Ted Jarrett. He had quite a few hit songs, even a couple of country songs he had written that were recorded by country artists, as well as songs that were covered by other famous groups like The Rolling Stones.

Ted wrote his autobiography called *You Can Make It If You Try*. Herbert is mentioned a lot in that book and appears in some big photos in the book, too. Before Ted died, he signed a copy of his book and gave it to me. Levert Allison, Gene Allison's brother, also sang on Jefferson Street in those days as part of that scene with Ted Jarrett and Gene Allison, and he is still a good friend. He's very supportive of the museum and what we're doing over here on Jefferson Street.

As the museum started to take hold, we had more and more musicians perform and share their stories. Lucius Talley, the drummer and spoons player, was an entertainer at the Jefferson Street Sound Museum along with many other Jefferson Street alumni musicians, including Marion James, Tina Brown, Saanea Jamison, Don Adams, Herbert O'Neil, and Doc Blakely.

Bit by bit over time, we began attracting attention from local and national media. An article in the *Tennessean* helped raise awareness of the museum's mission, as well as a Nashville Public Television documentary called "Facing North: Jefferson Street" which featured a segment about the museum. I was interviewed for a NewsChannel 5 piece called "From Nashville to Woodstock: Exploring Jimi Hendrix's History in Nashville" that aired and appeared online featuring the museum.

More and more people from Nashville, as well as tourists from around the world, started to come to the museum, and we received some wonderful testimonials and reviews from our guests. Some of my favorite online reviews called us "a gem of a spot," and "a true must if you want to know and feel Nashville's Soul history." Another reviewer wished some Black superstar like Oprah or Beyoncé would invest in "this hidden Black culture" because "our children need to know this history." Comments like that make all the hard work worth it. There's nothing I like better than sharing this rich history and seeing my visitors' eyes light up as they discover more about local history as well as the backstory of the famous people who got their start here.

One person who is now a close friend also helped promote the museum's mission and continues to support our work to this day. Rogers Hall is a professor at Vanderbilt University and a music-lover who grew up listening to the music that was created here on Jefferson Street without knowing where it came from. I met him at a reception at Vanderbilt he was running to present his work in designing learning spaces.

We had a mutual friend, Kim Johnson, who was working on developing the National Museum of African American Music, and she asked Jesse Boyce and me to attend so that she could introduce us to Rogers. Rogers had developed this really cool way of projecting an image that had QR codes built in so that people could walk through the image almost as if they were in the actual location. Then they could scan those codes to listen to music or watch videos about the location.

Rogers had been researching the history of Jefferson Street, so there Jesse and I stood, all dressed up for this fancy reception, looking at the old Jefferson Street map before the interstate tore it up, projected almost life-size on the wall. They were projecting our old stomping grounds, and we could stop off at any spot and watch a video about that place.

Just as Rogers and I got to talking and getting to know each other, I spotted a photo of myself dancing in one of the clubs. I couldn't have been more than 21 years old at the time.

"That's me!" I said to Rogers.

His eyes grew wide. "Oh my God!" was all he said. He wanted to know everything I could remember about those days on Jefferson Street, and we've been friends ever since. It was the beginning of what has been a wonderful partnership between Vanderbilt and the museum.

Rogers was running a summer course for ninth and tenth graders in the Vanderbilt summer academy. It was all about the untold stories and the history of Nashville. He brought the kids over to Jefferson Street on a boiling hot day to walk them around the neighborhood. Rogers hadn't been inside the museum yet, but I knew that was part of his plan for the day, so I was ready. Jesse was there waiting to talk to the kids with me, and the local rap artist we were recording in the studio came over to talk with them, too.

The kids looked like wilted flowers by the time they arrived at the front door, and I expected that. I had some big beach umbrellas set up and some ice chests full of ice-cold water for them. The doors were open, the AC was on, and I said, "Come on in, kids! Have some cold water!"

It was funny when Rogers told me later that he felt like I was the King of Jefferson Street in that moment.

It has been such a blessing to have university student teams visiting the museum on a regular basis. Rogers and Dave Owens, a professor in the business school, co-teach classes on learning design. Their students were on fire, building prototypes of what we would like to create for the museum. They would interview me and my family about our ideas and then create models to show how it could be done.

Rogers, his wife, Karen, and Dave Owens came over to join my family in tearing out some of the existing setups, and we spent a couple of weeks cleaning it up, painting it, and attaching monitors to the walls. Some of the ideas from the students' lab projects are now in that room, and it looks like a modern museum gallery with the monitors up on the walls.

In 2015, Vanderbilt's Space, Learning & Mobility Lab (SLaM) at Vanderbilt's Peabody College of Education and Human Development partnered with me to create what they call a

DSSL. That stands for a digital spatial story line. It's almost like the projection I first saw at the reception where I met Rogers, but this is done online in a digital app called StoryLiner. It's a very ambitious five-year project and it's funded by the National Science Foundation, called BLUES, which stands for Bridging Learning in Urban Extended Spaces. The project develops new ways for people to learn about the history of local, urban environments.

The Jefferson Street DSSL is an interactive map you can find online at slam.app.vanderbilt.edu. It is truly amazing work that these students did. They chose places all along the historic locations of Jefferson Street, and they found all kinds of photographs, oral histories, news articles, and song playlists collected from different sources, including the Nashville Public Library and the Country Music Hall of Fame and Museum. The students put it all together. It is inspiring to have a map of Historic Jefferson Street and be able to click anywhere on it and see old videos from the clubs, news footage of the Civil Rights marches going on in Nashville, and interviews with surviving artists from Jefferson Street's peak years.

"You can hold your mouse over a location on the map and hear Etta James sing at the New Era club, and then pick another spot and hear Jimi Hendrix play 'Purple Haze' at Club Baron," Rogers said. It's really something. The technology is way beyond me, but I have enjoyed clicking through their masterpiece. A lot of the students are excited to bring this kind of online learning experience to their own students after they graduate.

In 2016, Peabody College at Vanderbilt University, Department of Teaching and Learning, held a course called Inquiry in Education. They wanted to teach about community action and social change. Professor Andrew Hosteler used my work on Jefferson Street as an example of a community member who sees an opportunity or need to change something. He held classes and visited the museum with his students to learn more about my mission. It was inspiring to see the students so dedicated to the work of preserving an important legacy that was nearly lost. This was another step in our partnership with Vanderbilt that has been so rewarding for both our community and for the university.

I began to lead group tours of Jefferson Street, including the Chancellor's Charters tour for Vanderbilt University's Chancellor Zeppos. I was invited to speak for the Nashville Chapter of the Afro-American Historical and Genealogical Society. These were all huge honors to me.

Then in 2018, the Metropolitan Historical Commission presented me with the Preservation Achievement Award. The Achievement Award is given to an individual "in recognition of extraordinary leadership in preserving

Nashville's history – either through research and writing history, or through advocacy and raising public awareness of history and preservation," as the City government website says. And they gave it to me for what they called my "dedication to the documentation, preservation, and promotion of Jefferson Street's musical heritage."

A really fun experience was when Andrew Zimmern, the star of the Travel Channel's "Driven by Food" show, came to Nashville to visit Holly Williams, Hank Williams' granddaughter. Andrew had come to Nashville to film music and food. He said that universally, those two go together. Wherever you go in the world, you can bring music and food into the same room. When he came to Nashville, he wanted to know some of the music history. While they were riding in the van with a man they hired to show them around town, the driver told them about the famous musicians who played on Jefferson Street and recommended a stop at the museum.

When Holly Williams walked through the front door of the museum, the first thing she saw was her picture on the wall. It was the cover of a magazine that she was on. We just happened to have a small piece in that same magazine and that's why I had it on the wall. Jesse Boyce and I were featured in that magazine. Holly saw that picture and she and Andrew Zimmern just fell out laughing about that picture. She had never heard of Jefferson Street where all of this history lies. She was very excited to come into the building.

They stayed about four hours filming. Jesse Boyce was with me when they came in. When they got to speaking with Jesse, he started talking about disco music as part of the history of music. When Jesse mentioned the Saturday Night Band album we had made together, which was #2 on the national charts and got a Grammy nomination, Andrew said that he used to dance to that music at Club 54 in New York, so he knew the Saturday Night Band. That was exciting to hear. I had the album there in the museum, so I brought it out. Andrew was standing looking at the album and reminiscing about the fun that he had dancing to that Saturday Night Band song, "Come On, Dance, Dance."

After that, Andrew took everybody down to Ooh Wee Bar-B-Q next door and bought us all some barbeque because he was all about food and music. We ate barbeque together down at Ooh Wee's and had a great visit. The video he made is still archived on the Travel Channel site.

All the while, the collections kept growing at the museum. Marion James had contributed so much memorabilia and even gave me her own piano, the one she wrote all her tunes on, including her hit song "That's My Man." Family members of musicians who have passed on but who were part of that scene have donated all kinds of memorabilia and artifacts.

USA Today did a big article in 2021 called "Hallowed Sound: Artists Who Played a Role in the Former Jefferson Street Music District" about the museum. That has already helped bring more visitors to the museum and raise awareness of what we are doing here.

I am dedicated to improving and expanding the museum and its offerings every chance I get. At the same time, I keep looking for ways that the museum could continue to bless the community around me. I am always thinking and asking others, "What can we do to help revitalize Jefferson Street and bring music back here?"

Chapter 12
Our Vision for the Future of Jefferson Street

In front of the Jefferson Street Sound Museum

As I described to Brittany McKenna from the *Nashville Scene* (Dec. 28, 2016), "This is what God wanted to happen in this building. He wanted the history, and not only the history, but the future of the music, the sound and tones that are going to be part of the future, coming out of here, too. This is the capital of Nashville as far as R&B and blues music. It's Jefferson Street. I'm not no big nothing. I'm just a regular guy that God blessed with this idea."

I wanted to bring not only the memories back with the museum, but new music from the people of the neighborhood by producing and recording in the upstairs Jefferson Street Sound studio. I had a lot of ideas for how we could use this space to help revitalize the neighborhood.

Right now, Jefferson Street Sound is the only active record label here in the North Nashville area. I want to prove to the people of Nashville that the music business can come alive here again. I'm hoping to encourage more live music venues to open up here. After all, there is already so much redevelopment going on toward the east side of where we are, with Germantown and Salemtown, plus thousands of students attending our historically Black universities and colleges. The audience is already here, and if we can bring live music back as well as continue to grow the label and our recording artists, it should attract more and more investors, homeowners, and businesses back to Jefferson Street. That is my vision.

About five years ago, we began a revamping of the Jefferson Street Sound studio. In those five years, we have produced and recorded everything from song idea demos to complete albums. The studio has a dedicated engineer and is capable of recording whole groups at a time. We have a long list of great musicians who have recorded with us, including Stacy "Coffee" Jones and Teron "Bonafide" Carter (the members of the GRITS duo that has won Grammy and Dove awards), Writers Block, Larysa Jaye, and numerous local acts.

Our vision for the studio is to continue to be a staple recording location for up-and-coming artists and youth wanting to have a place in the rising "New Nashville," especially for those of color.

"This is a scene that is so vitally important not just to Jefferson Street, but to our city and our culture," I told an interviewer. It's already happening now on Jefferson Street – wherever there are a bunch of apartments or condos, the businesses start popping up: restaurants, furniture stores. You have to have businesses in a newly built community so you'll have something to support the homeowners who are buying all of these condos and homes.

I think Jefferson Street, moving into the future, could be overrun with new developments and see more businesses starting up. The businesses are only slowly coming to Jefferson Street because they haven't cleaned up the area enough. That's going to be a matter of time. I just hope our community will be able to survive the next round of revitalizing the area.

When I got started all the way up until now, I supported the museum financially myself. We have gotten a couple of small grants recently, but for 10 years or so, I solely supported the museum, buying one picture at a time, mounting the pictures on the wall. In the beginning, nobody hung pictures on the wall but me. Pretty much everything that has been done up until now has been managed by me, but friends and family have stepped up to help at critical times, too.

Now I have Tracey and Ryan helping with administrative tasks, and when it comes to the technology, they handle all that. I'm not technologically inclined. I am so glad to have them with me on this journey, sharing my vision for the museum with them. They have brought more and more value to the community with their ideas and skills. It is a very special and gratifying experience to have my kids grow to adults and be an instrumental part of the future of Jefferson Street Sound Museum.

My son Ryan is the Executive Director who handles the technical aspects of the museum by maintaining an upgraded website that includes a donation campaign and offering the purchase of merchandise through a third-party source. He also seeks funding for the museum through grant opportunities. Through the museum, he also started providing financial literacy courses in 2019, partnering with more nonprofits in the Nashville metro area. He has been developing programs to benefit the community and help empower youth to understand their financial future and possibilities.

Other projects of Ryan's at the museum include community yoga, meditation, and breath work classes. Using the Jefferson Street Sound motto, "Back in the Day, Shaping Tomorrow," we are working to shape the future of the community through life skills training and self-awareness education. The lost history of Jefferson Street is what we want to honor by showing the opportunities of where it could go, to help the community decide how it wants to go forward, and to create a safe space for the community.

We will also be doing a Tiny History Desk series – live events JSSM hosts to present local artists and musicians who haven't had a chance to get in the spotlight. We are also hosting live concerts via social media and integrating that with interviews with individuals about Jefferson Street history back in the day.

The JSSM scholarship fund is another project that has helped teens learn money management and how to empower themselves using money and resources. We want to bring more awareness around generating wealth for themselves and their families. The scholarship fund will resume in 2022 after fundraising efforts.

My daughter Tracey is the Executive Director of Event Planning. She plans all the events for JSSM internally and externally and handles all of the administrative duties. She put together the JSSM Community Outreach Day on July 18th, 2020. We had an awesome time that day. With our

Voters Registration drive, we registered 5 people to vote. We awarded the winner of the JSSM Scholarship Fund $200 and awarded three other participants $100 each. We gave away food, baby diapers, sanitary supplies for women, clothes, and household items to around 100 people in the North Nashville area.

At that event, we also had a mental health booth to distribute materials on mental health awareness and how to contact mental health professionals. A contractor working in the area saw our mental health booth and gave a small donation because there were mental health issues in her family. That was touching and it made us feel great about the work we were doing. We also did a drawing and gave away gift cards throughout the day donated by my son Dwayne Lewis's church, New Season Church.

All of these special programs and events are just the beginning of the many things we want to continue to do to support the rebirth of Jefferson Street and our precious community. For quite some time, I have been working hard with others in the community to convince the City of Nashville to put what is now the Elks Lodge on the historic register. It's the only building left standing on Jefferson Street that housed an original Black music venue. Back in the day, that building was the site of Club Baron, where Jimi Hendrix and Johnny Jones had their guitar duel and Johnny took Jimi to school. That's where Little Richard performed his big hit 'Tutti Frutti." A host of other famous artists and musicians played over the years at Club Baron until it closed in the '60s.

It was an uphill battle, but our perseverance paid off. Getting the Elks Lodge building on the historic register is just the first victory in what I see as a long road ahead to restore Jefferson Street to its proper status as a musical and cultural center in our city. I've never allowed defeat to stop me, and I've been defeated a number of times – so many, many times. But none of those defeats have stopped me. Here I am now, 78 years old here, talking about writing a book. I never thought I'd get to this point. I couldn't read, so how would I write a book? It took so much of what I felt I didn't have in order to put a book together. But, you know, who ever thought that I would be a part of producing a nationally known hit record or making a soap for McDonald's that could have been sold around the world? Put no limitations on how far you can go in life. It just depends on your desire.

One of my biggest desires has always been to be wealthy, to be comfortable. I had the big house with the swimming pool and all of that. But this is where God has got me now – he blessed me with the duties of preserving a legacy, the legacy of all of these great musicians and artists who have been a part of Jefferson Street in Nashville, Tennessee.

That's what God has assigned me to do, and I'm determined to do the best I can on this assignment.

Acknowledgments

I owe great thanks to my friends Rogers Hall, Lionel Barrett, Dr. Morgan Hines, and Terry Selman for their continued support over the years.

I could not be who I am today without my brothers and cousins, and especially my mother, Julia Washington.

I would also like to thank all these important people for the part they played in making this journey a success: Agnes Scott, Michael and Erlene Jones, Barbara Woods Washington, Martin Bennett, Jim Caden, Ingrid Fletcher, Eugene Campbell, Milton Cortner, Asieren Boyce, Gwendolyn Smith, Wanda Walker-Battle, Marion James and the Musician's Aid Society, Richard Manson, Michael Gray, Jarrel Pierson, Tim Walker, and Albert Collins.

I would like to thank all the Vanderbilt professors and students who worked on the project presenting the sights and sounds of Nashville's Historic Jefferson Street. It is an amazing compilation of stories, photos, audio recordings, and videos about the music and civil rights history of our beloved community, and I hope you will check it out and enjoy it at https://slam.app.vanderbilt.edu.

To the staff of Living Legends Media and Newbern Consulting, I want to say thank you for helping to make this book possible. Your hard work and diligence have not gone unnoticed.

Finally, to my daughter Tracey, I owe much gratitude for her perseverance and dedication to making my story a family legacy.

Any time you are in Nashville, please visit us at:
Jefferson Street Sound Museum
2004 Jefferson Street
Nashville, TN 37208
615-414-6675 • www.jeffersonstreetsound.com

Running the Soul Shack in the '70s

With my daughter Tracey, my son Ryan, my mother Julia Washington, and brother Ernest Washington at Tracey's college graduation

With Marion James, Nashville's Queen of the Blues

Don Adams, bass player, songwriter, and arranger

Lucius "Spoonman" Talley in front of the Jefferson Street Sound Museum mural of Jimi Hendrix and Billy Cox

With my son Dwayne Lewis at his daughter Markisha's wedding

With Rogers Hall, Karen Wieckert from Vanderbilt, and my son Dwayne Lewis

With my daughter Tracey Washington at the Delta Sigma Theta Christmas Party

With my son Ryan Washington

With my sons Ryan Washington and Dwayne Lewis, and my daughter Tracey Washington

Reminiscing with Watt Watson (bass guitarist) at the Tennessee State Museum

An original guitar of Jimi Hendrix's that he smashed and had refurbished (not displayed in the museum)

With Levert Allison (a musical artist with the group Fairfield Four) and Watt Watson (bass guitarist)

Leading a walking tour down Historic Jefferson Street

My son Dwayne's family, with all his children and grandchildren

My son Ryan and his daughter Alanni

Jefferson Street Sound

BACK IN THE DAY - SHAPING TOMORROW

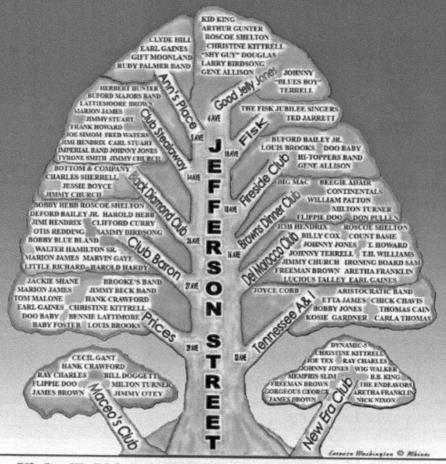

Night Clubbin' on HISTORICAL Jefferson Street

Back in the Day- 1940's - 1970's

Nashville, Tennessee

Website: jeffersonstreetsound.com